Escape the Rat Race

with Property Lease Options

Barry Davies

Mozaique Publishing
Carmarthenshire UK

First published in paperback 2013 by Mozaique Publishing

ISBN 978-0-9576277-0-3

A CIP catalogue record for this book is available from the British Library.

There is a hardcopy version of this book available on Amazon, from the author or to order from all good bookstores.

Contents

Foreword

As the founder of the property investors network, the UK's largest and fastest growing network of property investing specific network meetings, I have the pleasure of meeting thousands of property investors every year.

I first met Barry Davies in 2009 when he joined my twelve-month Property Mastermind Programme. During the programme Barry mastered the art of creating great cash-flow, through properties he didn't own using leases and lease options. This is probably the fastest strategy for generating great cash-flow with no need for a mortgage or deposit.

Barry has built a multi-million pound property portfolio which generates thousands of pounds in income every month and he now helps others to do the same. He speaks regularly on my Property Mastermind Programme and gets great results. Rather than just giving information, he encourages the delegates to actually get on the phone there and then, often with the result that they walk away with a deal lined up. I'm very selective about who I work with and who I will put in front of my students. Barry is generous with his knowledge and he gets results and that's why I like working with him.

In this book "Escape the Rat Race", Barry gives a great insight into what it takes to be successful investor. He shares his inspiring story of how he started with nothing except a great attitude and overcame many hurdles to get to where he is today. The book includes many real life case studies of how he and his students have secured high value properties in affluent areas using leases and lease options and then let them out room by room to maximise cash-flow to generate £500-£1,000 per month per property.

In each case study the seller's motivation for selling this way is explained and this gives the reader great examples, which they can model to ethically influence other sellers to do the same. Barry demonstrates how it is possible to create win-win deals to secure properties being sold by even the most wealthy and financially astute landlords such as solicitors and accountants. This strategy has also been proven in major cities in the south of England which many people would think would be hard to conquer.

Unlike many other books "Escape the Rat Race" also gives step-by-step practical advice about how to manage your property business and tenants to realise the high cash-flow month after month. After all, getting a great deal is only half the battle. Escape the Rat Race is a great book for anyone who wants to use Lease

Options to build a high cash-flow portfolio without the need for a deposit. It has been a pleasure to mentor and work with Barry over the last few years and I look forward to witnessing his growing success in the future.

Kind regards,

Simon Zutshi
Author of "Property Magic"
Founder property investors network
www.pinmeeting.co.uk

Introduction

I am passionate about property and about business; building a property portfolio and developing it into a property business has been an amazing journey with many highs and lows. My journey has made me grow both as a businessman and a person. I am not talking of nice steady growth where you calmly learn and then slowly implement. Some of the biggest growth has come from the biggest adversities that forced my business partner and I to rise to the challenge or go bankrupt.

I am writing this book to inspire and educate people to invest in property. This can be done by anyone with the right attitude. I started with £7,500 and now have a multi-million pound portfolio that pays me whether I work or not. I now have staff that manage and maintain my portfolio with little input from me. I now have the privilege of spending my time working on bigger deals and sharing my knowledge and experience with others. I am in the fortunate position where I could retire but the idea couldn't be further from my mind. I love what I do and don't really consider it work. Life is about continually growing, learning and contributing.

To your success!

Getting the Best Out of This Book

This book has been split into sections. The first details my story including some of the deals that my mentoring clients and I have done using leases and lease option contracts. I have done my best to explain them step by step. However if you are completely new to property investment and do not understand lease option contracts it may be best to read Part 3 first to familiarise yourself with the basics.

There are case studies throughout this book. After each one I have left space for you to make notes to aid your learning. Please use these spaces to detail what you have learnt from each that you can use to help you build your own portfolio. At the back of this book I have also included an action sheet for you to list the actions you will take to move your property investing forward. The more actively you read this book (by making notes as you go) the more you will learn and achieve.

Extra Online Resources

To receive my Options Deal Calculator to help you calculate exactly how to construct an offer, please email me at barry@barrydaviesproperty.co.uk with the words 'Option Deal Calculator' in the title of the email.

Part 1: My Story

The Highlights
(and Low-Points)

Chapter 1: "You're Fired"

"Getting fired, despite sometimes coming as a surprise and leaving you scrambling to recover, is often a godsend. Most people aren't lucky enough to get fired and die a slow spiritual death over 30-40 years of tolerating the mediocre."

Tim Ferriss

By far the best day I spent at Airbus was the day I was fired. I've never had such a feeling of freedom and elation as that moment when I walked out of the door for the last time. The future couldn't have been less certain, I had no idea how I would pay the mortgage and credit card bills and yet I couldn't have frowned if I had tried; my jaw was aching by the end of the day from my incessant grin. Apparently our property company was infringing on company time, the rest is history.

It's disappointing really, the company makes the best aircraft using world-leading technology and yet most employees had no passion. In fact, I think I'd go as far as to say that most of the people there were either robots or already half dead. Smiles on Monday morning were as rare as rocking-horse shit; it literally took people until Friday to smile, and they only smiled then because they got to escape again for a couple of days. I always used to think that there must be more to life than this; surely living for the weekend was nonsensical? There are only two days in the weekend and five during the week. Living for the weekend meant wasting nearly three-quarters of the week!

I do not blame them for firing me, I would never have anyone working for me who did not want to be there, and their decision was the push I needed. I wonder what made them twig – was it the smile? Was it because I only wore a suit on the days I was meeting estate agents after work? The fact that I was wearing a suit to that place still makes me chuckle, most people start to dress up when they want a promotion. This was the furthest thing from my mind and as it turned out – the feeling was mutual.

The disciplinary process itself was rather amusing. Ben my best mate and partner-in-crime was in a disciplinary of his own. We had both worked at Airbus for ten years and received an extra day's holiday for the length of service. Big deal! Ben was shown a copy of the resignation letter he had previously typed on his work computer and then e-mailed to me: our bosses had apparently requested the IT department to trawl through our emails. He had written it to inspire us months earlier as we both wanted to leave the company as soon as we had enough money coming in from our property ventures. I'm sure he never thought he'd have to explain it to his boss! I talk light heartedly about the situation now, but I've been on a roller coaster ride since that day. Carving out your own journey rather than following the norm takes balls. With an income of only - £50 (minus) a month it takes balls of steel!

We had just re-mortgaged the first house we'd renovated together and pulled out £17,000 (equivalent to five months combined salary after tax). We had to act fast, there was a very real risk that we could lose everything, but what would we do? The first thing I did was to write a letter to my boss entitled 'Thanks for the push!' The letter was post-dated for one year later; it thanked him and explained that I now had a million pound property portfolio that paid me £50,000 a year. Obviously it was more of a letter to myself than to him, however, the process of writing it down on paper was very powerful!

Chapter 2: Baptism of Fire – The Flats

Looking back, I have been interested in property for as long as I can remember. Some of my first memories are of following my dad around the house whilst he was doing DIY. Whether it was building some wardrobes or erecting a six foot fence, I was always there. I bought my first house by default. I still lived at home and my mum was moving on; I didn't want to move so the logical thing to do was to buy the house from her. She kindly offered to gift my sister and I a 10% deposit. I didn't really think about this at the time but this was my first purchase and I did it using none of my own money! A sure sign of things to come.

The house didn't really need much work, I was in my early twenties and socialising was my main concern so I decided to lay a big patio and build a brick BBQ for my friends and me. It was during this time that I read my first self-development book, "The Midas Method" by Stuart Goldsmith. The book was very simple and yet profound, the author described how you could achieve anything you chose. This was not what I had been taught at school and certainly not the view of the vast majority of the population. The idea really resonated with me. Why should I settle for the mediocre? Why shouldn't I be one of those people with an extraordinary life who loved what they did every day? This was a lovely thought and yet I wasn't sure how I would get there.

I had always wanted to buy and refurbish properties and had thought that this would be a great way to supplement my income. It was 2005; we had now been paying off our mortgage for two years and had paid off a whopping £4,000 – hardly ground breaking! Luckily, during the same period the property value had increased by £40,000. I was eager to get my teeth into a project as my job wasn't inspiring me. I decided that it was time to get into property!

I re-mortgaged the house and withdrew £20,000. I thought it would be easy to find a property that I could make some money on. Everyone seemed to be doing it; Property Ladder was one of the most popular programmes on TV. I searched high and low for a suitable property but the competition was massive. If the value of a property would be worth £150,000 once refurbished, it would usually sell for £140,000 and probably need £10,000 worth of work. This made no sense whatsoever; essentially you would end up doing the work for nothing. At the time prices were going through the roof but I didn't want to rely on that. I knew that price rises wouldn't last forever and I wanted to maximise my financial gain by creating value through the refurbishment process. If I made money from a rising market I wanted this to be a bonus rather than a necessity.

Over the next eighteen months I offered on about twenty-five properties to no avail − I was always a couple of grand short of what others were willing to pay. The closest I came was with a flat above a Co-op shop. The property consisted of a large reception room, one double bedroom, a bathroom and a kitchen. The reception room was four metres by five metres which seemed excessive for a one-bedroom flat. I realised that I could put the kitchen into the front room and still have space for both a living area and a dining area, allowing me to add a second bedroom where the kitchen used to be. There was a lot of interest and so the seller (the Co-op) instructed all interested parties to put their bids into a sealed envelope by a certain time on a certain date. It should have been an exciting process but having been outbid so many times over the previous eighteen months I was pretty numb to the process. I was delighted when I found out that I was the highest bidder. I was eager to get started, I had been waiting a long time and the money was burning a hole in my pocket. A week later I had the disappointing news that the seller had pulled out. I was gutted and a little confused, why would a large company like Co-op go to the trouble of putting the property on the market only to pull out a month later? A little while later I found out that Co-op and Somerfield had merged and the whole building was sold. So, back to the drawing board.

I was more than a little disappointed but I always look for the positives. This process had taught me something − if you add to a property then you can add value. In this case I had realised a way to add an extra bedroom and therefore I could offer a higher bid than other parties and still make a profit. I started to look for properties where I could add value rather than just restoring the existing layout. During my search I realised that three-bedroom houses in a given area were selling for £150,000-£160,000 whereas one-bedroom flats were selling for £100,000-£120,000. I did some sums and believed I could complete a conversion of a house into two flats for about £30,000, therefore I would stand to make almost £40,000 profit. E.g. (£110,000 + £115,000 = £225,000 value of the two flats - £157,000 paid for house - £28,000 spent on conversion = £40,000 profit).

Realising this was a great breakthrough, I immediately started viewing two- to three-bedroom houses and putting offers forward. I had an offer accepted and was delighted. I pushed the sale through as quickly as possible as I didn't want to lose another opportunity, I was glad to exchange and complete the transaction five to six weeks later!

It didn't enter my head that I may have some trouble with the works, even though £30,000 was a tight budget meaning that I would have to do the majority of the work myself. I had built a BBQ in my previous house and helped my uncle fit my mum's kitchen when I was 14 years old, surely there couldn't be that much more to it? A lot of people didn't think I was realistic and thought it was ridiculous − those people still have jobs that they don't like. I detest the word 'realistic'. It is probably the most limiting word in the English language. I use online dictionaries now but if I still had a hard copy I would remove the word realistic. Will Smith said in an interview:

"it's unrealistic to think you're going to bend a piece of metal and fly people over the ocean in that metal, that's unrealistic but fortunately the Wright brothers and others didn't believe that."

Will Smith

Please search YouTube for 'Will Smith's Wisdom' to see a great compilation of his interviews, he shares some great philosophy.

http://www.youtube.com/watch?v=DSEV6O5JoPI

Anyway back to the story ... With my new found knowledge on the potential profit achievable by converting houses to flats I was keener than ever. I was probably a bit too keen, because rather than waiting for a house in need of renovation that I could get more cheaply I just bought a house in average condition and paid full market value for it. I applied for planning permission and one of the adjoining neighbours made every possible objection they could think of. Luckily planning officers pay more attention to planning guidelines than to neighbours with a "not in my back yard" attitude. I got the decision just before Christmas and decided to celebrate by knocking a wall down with a big sledge hammer. Boys will be boys, hey!

At this point I wasn't over every hurdle − the planning department had informed me that I still had to comply with building regulations. The relevant drawings were done by a Structural Engineer friend and forwarded to the building control department, who stated that they were happy with the fire and sound proofing provisions and simply asked that we prove that the current structure was capable of carrying the extra weight. I called my Structural Engineer asking him to provide the calculations. Three hours later he called back, sounding worried, and said that he had redone the calculations three times and realised that the floor wasn't strong enough. He suggested replacing all of the timbers holding up the first floor. The problem was that I had already rewired the flats – and the cables ran right through the centre of every joist. I racked my brains, there had to be another way. Money was tight, my contingency was almost non-existent. In the end I came up with the solution of using steel columns and joists to support the ceiling from beneath. The building inspector approved the solution and I breathed a sigh of relief. This was the first (and worst) of many hurdles that I would have to overcome. Everything I did took twice as long as I expected and because of my inexperience some of the jobs needed to be done twice where I had made mistakes. Eventually the work was completed.

I had been working thirty-five to forty hours in my job and then forty to fifty hours on site, evenings and weekends. I had been flat out working and barely had time to think of anything else but even I couldn't avoid what had happened in the global financial market. My costs had also risen by £2,000. Initially I was expecting to make £40,000 on the project but the market had changed. It was time to invite the surveyor round to enable me to re-mortgage the property to withdraw funds for the next project. I was more than a little nervous, all of my hard work for the last year rested on the surveyor's valuation, I knew the property market had crashed but didn't want to believe it. I knew this would affect the valuation negatively but I wasn't sure by how much. After all this hard work I really wanted to make a profit even if it was a small profit.

There was a knock at the door: it was the surveyor. I let him in. He was pleasant enough but not giving much away – a real 'poker face'. I had done all I could, now it was just a waiting game. A couple of days later whilst I was weight training in the garden with a couple of friends when the phone rang, it was the mortgage broker. Rather than being worth the £225,000 that the agent had suggested a year earlier, the combined value was £180,000. Rather than making a profit of £40,000 if I had sold the flats then I would have lost £7,000 as my total cost including the work was £187,000.

I had worked eighty to ninety hours a week; I had given up most of my social life and had foregone any holiday for over a year. I was now worse off than before, worse off financially than if I had spent every weekend in the pub and had been on two or three weeks' holiday like most of my friends. The only mortgage available was at 6.8%, meaning that keeping the flats and renting them out would make me a very small profit every month. That was a very low point. I was absolutely gutted. I always had the belief that if you work hard you would get rewarded, yet on this project I had worked my balls off and felt that my reward was a big slap in the face. Most people would have given up here but in the words of Winston Churchill "*Never give in, never, never, never ... give in*". That low point lasted a good couple of hours until I pulled myself together. I realised that regardless of what had happened in the market, what I had achieved that year was great and what I had learnt was invaluable. Based on that valuation I would still be able to re-mortgage the flats and withdraw £15,000 because I had invested so much in the deposit and the refurbishment. This amount was just about enough to fight another battle! Please forgive the rather abrupt end to this story. As you will learn as you read through the rest of this book, I don't like to dwell on the negative.

The next battle was a small Victorian terrace, which I bought with my best friend Ben. We did this because we needed to pool funds to move forward; neither of us could afford both the deposit and the money to improve the property. It had previously sold for £150,000, and we thought we had done really well to get it for £101,000 after it had been repossessed from the previous owner. During the refurbishment we found rising damp throughout the ground floor of the property. This meant that the plaster had to be removed from every wall of the ground floor, the walls needed to be injected with a damp proofing agent and then the plaster needed to be replaced. Unfortunately, both the kitchen and bathroom were located on the ground floor which meant that these also needed to be removed. We also found rotten timbers under the ground floor and the dreaded dry rot in the loft caused by a previous leak. This was work that we hadn't fully anticipated.

At this time we were reading a lot of property books and attending various property seminars. We kept hearing that the most valuable thing we could do was to find property deals and that we should get others to do the refurbishment for us. We were unsure about this because paying others to do the work significantly increased our costs and reduced our profit. However we listened to the advice and did very little of the work ourselves. This pushed our refurbishment cost up from £10,000 to £17,000. We were now set to make £7,000 less profit because we had paid to get the work done. We had estimated that the property would be worth £130,000 to £135,000 when the work was completed based on comparable market data and we were disappointed when the mortgage valuation came back at £125,000, meaning that we made a £7,000 profit. The problem was that the mortgage company knew that we had bought it for £101,000 and surveyors were under a lot of pressure to remain cautious regarding valuations because the property market was uncertain and some banks were concerned about further price falls. Despite this we were able to refinance the property based on the

£125,000 valuation; however, this allowed us to raise only £17,000. Our investment capital was decreasing and we knew we would need more funds in order to continue investing.

Chapter 3: Our First Seminar

We had been investing in our education and during the previous year we had learnt a lot about property. We really wanted to help others see the benefit of property investment and felt we could make some money from doing this. Just before being given the boot from Airbus we had put on a seminar for the few people we knew that were interested in investing in property. There were about fifteen people in the room; at least half were family but it was great to have the moral support! We found one investor who actually had a deposit, and couldn't believe our luck! He was willing to pay us to find a property with a 20-25% discount. The investor was the brother of another Airbus employee who was keen to escape the rat race and was becoming our first fan. The discount was still hard to find but at least we didn't need to do anything creative with the financing. We found him a flat worth around £80,000 that we were able to get for £62,000. The investor was French and working in Germany, so as long as we could get over the hurdles that international mortgages presented we were home and dry. The mortgage was approved and the solicitors were almost finished with their part so the investor sent us his deposit ready for completion.

Chapter 4: Our Time was Running Out

We had now been self-employed for nearly six months and to be fair things could have been going a lot better. The days were long; we were leafleting six or seven hours per day (actually going out and traipsing round the streets rather than employing someone as we were skint) as well as spending an eight-hour day in the office to do all the more enjoyable things around setting up a business and viewing properties with estate agents then plucking up the courage to make an offer of 70-75% of its value.

The worst thing was we were starting to get skinny; no man wants to be skinny, least of all a rugby player. The only joy in leafleting was seeing Ben get chased out of the gardens by dogs. The scariest dogs were the silent ones – silent at least until they hit the other side of the front door at 40mph with a massive BANG! That is the funniest thing ever, unless it happens to you! Then it's enough to stop your heart beating for a second or two!

Our success was very limited; maybe lack of experience had something to do with it but I suspect it was the fact that we were trying to do 'no money down' deals like everyone else and it just didn't sit well with us. The processes being employed to purchase the properties were questionable; typically a property was bought at 70-75% of its value but somehow the sale was put through to the mortgage company at full market value effectively creating the deposit out of thin air. I fully appreciate that buyers using this method are doing a relatively good thing by helping sellers to avoid repossessions, etc. At the same time it did feel slightly fraudulent, and I really feel that by doing something outside of our normal values we were making things difficult for ourselves and somehow causing deals to fall over.

Money was running out fast, we were down to our last £1,500 and something needed to change. Everyone was telling us to get a job. The thought of this made me feel sick, I felt like all of our efforts would have been in vain. I also felt that if I settled into a job I may never leave again now I knew how hard it was to make it on your own. If you're ever in this position and need inspiration watch the Sylvester Stallone story told by Anthony Robbins on YouTube.

http://www.youtube.com/watch?v=5tknowAM50Y&feature=fvst

Luckily the thought of getting a job made me feel even more sick than the porridge I was eating two or three times a day to save money and to stop me from wasting away whilst leafleting for six to eight hours every day.

Chapter 5: The Winning Strategy – Our First Break

The change finally came when we heard about a strategy on Simon Zutshi's Mastermind programme, which we had joined just prior to being sacked. The strategy was really simple: you lease a property from a landlord paying them market rent, then let the property out room by room to students or professionals with the owner's consent. By doing this it is possible to achieve 30-50% more rent and this uplift is your profit. For example:

Large multi-bedroomed house
Rent / Lease to landlord = £1,000
Number of rooms = 5
Rent per room = £300 (exclusive of bills)
Total rent = £1,500
Profit = £500

We found a couple of properties through local agents and went to view them. Despite never having bought or run a house-share before we convinced them we knew what we were doing. The agents just seemed pleased that we were no longer viewing properties for sale and only offering 70-75% of what they were worth.

We were really excited when two landlords agreed to lease us their properties, we got straight to work furnishing the houses. This concept had to work; we were using our last bit of money for furniture and agency fees. Ben started frantically looking for tenants. Our first tenant arrived a little too quickly; we had been given access to the properties for viewings and so on, but the paperwork had not been completed. We felt really guilty and agreed that the tenant could stay with us in the house we had just finished refurbishing and were still living in, for the three-four days until the rental house was ready and the paperwork signed.

Chapter 6: The Big Con

In the meantime our tenant, named Mark, was at a loose end and offered to give us a hand with the rest of the furniture, etc. He said his dad was a landlord and he was full of great advice. We thought it was strange that he was so helpful; maybe he just really appreciated us helping him out with accommodation? We were too busy to think about it too much. Having two big houses to fill with both students and furniture is no mean feat on a shoestring! We filled the houses and were super-pleased with ourselves. Mark had given us some reason or another not to move into either of the houses. He had decided to get a waterfront apartment instead. He had been with us for a couple of weeks now and hadn't put his hand in his pocket at all, but we hadn't minded giving him food and so on because he was working for us nearly full time for free.

Three months earlier we had booked a trip to Rome to see the motivational speaker Anthony Robbins. Always very optimistic, we had booked because we expected to be rolling in cash by the time we went! Mark our new tenant had become our friend and agreed to come with us to Rome; he was due to get a later flight and meet us there. After we had got to Rome and were having dinner just down the road from our hotel, something wasn't quite adding up about Mark's story. I can't remember what it was now, but I had a sinking feeling when I realised that we had left someone we hardly knew in our house. I realised that Mark would have had access to our bank cards and details during the time he was living with us. I quickly phoned the bank who confirmed my fears - my bank details had been used on the phone and the internet. I cancelled my cards and didn't know what to do. Should I go home to find out what was going on? Or stay in Rome for what I had been told by so many was a life changing experience? We decided to stay in Rome and face the music when we got back, reassuring ourselves that we would be better equipped to deal with the situation after four days with the world's leading peak performance coach.

The event was amazing: it is hard to describe it to anyone who has not been through it. On the first day you walk on hot coals. This really shifts your thinking; if you can walk on hot burning coals you can do anything! This set the scene for the weekend. These events really help you overcome whatever is holding you back and help you to create what you want in your life. They are not for the faint-hearted though, they are very American and happy-clappy. It is a bit of a shock to the system when you walk in on the first day and everyone is dancing and jumping around. It runs through your head that everyone might have been drinking but this was in the morning on a school day. They weren't drunk, just crazy! Crazy in a good 'full of life' way. You know when somebody who is very positive and has lots of energy walks into a room and brightens it up? The room was full of these people! It was a far cry from the dull office that used to be part of my life. You will have to just trust me and go to one of these events. We left an amazing event where we had made many great friends and grown closer to the friends we went with.

It was time to fly home to face the music. We were not sure what we would be going back to. Would Mark still be at the house? Would we have a house left? Would he have cleared out the entire house? What would we say to him? Would we call the police? We still had no concrete proof that it was him who had used the card details. What would he say when we confronted him? Would there be a fight? Then what? We were quite nervous as the taxi pulled up to our street. All the lights were off so we took a deep breath and opened the door. He wasn't there, but the house was immaculately clean which was a little eerie as we had been so busy with the student houses working twelve to fourteen hour days that our house had become rather messy. His clothes were still there; would he be back? I checked his bag and his passport was still there too, surely he wouldn't have left that if he was going to do a runner? Ben came to the conclusion that the cleaning was the behaviour of a guilty man.

We heard a key turn in the lock. Was it a coincidence that he was back three minutes after our return? We confronted him; he denied it and said it must have been someone else who had got my card details. We had no solid proof and it was late so we asked him to leave and agreed to meet in the morning. After he left we found some of the things that had been bought using my cards: an Xbox and some golf clubs. We were angry but more than that we were confused. What sort of con man would buy such things and then leave them at the property of the person he had defrauded? He had had every chance to leave and take not only the things he'd bought fraudulently but also our computers and laptops, stereo, DVD player, etc. He had also helped us in the business for two weeks for free. Confused and disillusioned, we decided to get some sleep. The Anthony Robbins event had been great and we were exhausted from the nonstop fourteen hour days.

I awoke early and went through the online account. We were £2,500 down in total. How was this possible if we had already been down to our last £1,500? Well, some of the money we were defrauded of belonged to the investor for whom we were buying the house. We were new to investing and knew nothing of client accounts back then. We had a house to buy for an investor and not enough money to buy it with. We had been open, helpful and trying to do someone a favour by letting him stay in our home. How did we deserve this? It all seemed so unfair. Both Ben and I believe that, generally, if you are good to people they will be good to you. If there was a lesson that some higher power was trying to teach us, we didn't have a clue what it was.

We met Mark at 10.00am in the city centre and when we confronted him with the evidence there was no way he could deny it. He held his hands up, apologised and said that he had made up a story because he had wanted us to like him. He told us that he had spoken to his dad, confessed all, and his dad was going to transfer the money. He would meet us later. We didn't know what to do. Should we just call the police? We knew there was only a small chance we would get that money from him but we needed it urgently. We knew that going through the police would take more time than we had. We decided to give him a chance, more out of pure desperation than anything else; we really needed that money.

Needless to say we never saw Mark again. We went to the police and Mark was well known to them. He was a convicted fraudster and since he had come back out of prison he was wanted on seven other counts of fraud including, of all things, trying to steal a plane!

We both still feel rather puzzled about his motives whenever we think about the incident. He left our lives with less than he entered. Now he didn't even have a passport. It was a sad case – perhaps he had been doing it to make himself feel significant. What an awful way to live. I hope he can sort things out. I imagine he's probably playing mummies and daddies with some bigger boys in prison by now.

Chapter 7: Sink or Swim

"Do not pray for easier lives. Pray to be stronger men!"

J F Kennedy

The phone call to our investor was probably the worst call I've ever had to make. I assured him that although I didn't know how we would do it, we would return his money. It was sink or swim time so I pulled the last available funds out of my four credit cards, thus 'maxing them out'. We had just enough to cover the investor's portion of the money that had been taken. We had passed the first hurdle but now we had squeezed every account dry and had no backup plan. Winston Churchill once said "If you're going through hell, keep going". The only way through this was to grow as a business and as people. We dug deep inside ourselves. This may sound brave but it wasn't; it was simpler than that, we had no other choice.

On the positive side we now had a business model that worked – leasing properties and renting them out room by room. It was simple but effective. Now we faced an even bigger challenge: we had to grow with no immediate funds. Our belief in ourselves kept us going.

We scoured the Internet for a property that was furnished so we wouldn't have to buy furniture. We found the property to let on Gumtree (we couldn't afford the £200-£300 agency fee). The property did turn out to be advertised by an agent. We met the agent and she was happy to proceed but most importantly there was no mention of an agency fee. I hoped if I just kept my mouth shut she might forget. Luckily she forgot right up to the time when we signed the lease. We paid by cheque and quickly gathered the rent and deposits from the tenants.

We were on a roll and quickly agreed another lease. Ben was getting great at marketing and we had eight people turn up for the viewing; three of them agreed to rent rooms! That was enough to cover the lease fee. Then the landlady pulled out without giving a reason. We had taken holding deposits and felt really bad for the tenants. Within twenty-four hours we had found another property. The letting agents were stricter this time. They wanted the funds cleared in their accounts before giving us the keys. Somehow, we had to get the money from the new tenants without giving them the keys. What's more, the agency insisted on a deposit equivalent to six weeks' rent. This would eat up all of the first month's profit until we got it back at the end of the lease. Needing this extra bit of funds also meant that we needed six tenants to all meet at the same time.

Anyone that has managed a HMO will know that this is nigh on impossible, especially during office hours. We crossed our fingers and agreed to meet all the tenants in a coffee shop just around the corner from the letting agent. This had to work as there was no other option. We were honest with the tenants about what was happening and luckily they trusted us. We both breathed a massive sigh of relief. We had done it! On paper we were financially free – provided we never went out to eat or drink, took no holidays, nothing ever went wrong with the houses, and we had no voids/vacancies. Obviously we still had a long way to go but this was a massive achievement for us. Following this success we quickly filled seven other houses, five of them in just one month. That was some stressful month!

Since that time the strategy has become known as the Ben and Barry strategy. Many have copied it and some even tried to make out that they invented it. This strategy has been around for years but we were the first to take it and later package it into a great one day educational seminar.

Chapter 8: Our First Option Deal

So we were now financially free! Yes we had some debt but we were now in a position to service that debt. We could even afford to stop eating like students and could pop out to the pub occasionally (previously this was confined to Christmas and Birthdays). We both breathed a huge sigh of relief but didn't rest for long. We now had momentum! We were on a roll and wanted to keep it going. I had always been keen to build a portfolio that I owned. We had learnt that option contracts are a way to control property in a similar way to the leases that we had already done successfully. This new contract would allow us to buy the properties in the future at a pre-agreed price. This seemed like a great way to get started since we didn't have money for a deposit and were not sure we could get a mortgage on the large properties that we had our eyes on.

Ben and I were on our way back from another Simon Zutshi Mastermind workshop. We were starving hungry. We'd been weight training in the gym about three times a week which meant we were always famished. Generally we would eat five or six times a day but that wasn't easy to do on a course. We had left

Birmingham about 6.00pm and it was now around 7.30pm. We stopped at a Chinese and ordered a takeaway; we were so hungry that we were both very irritable. Whilst waiting, we started to flick through a newspaper to distract ourselves from our hunger when we came across the 'Property to Let' section. We remembered back to the afternoon Mastermind session where we had been told to call landlords who were advertising properties for rent with a view to sourcing option deals. We ripped the number out and thought nothing more of it – until we found it on Monday morning when we thought:

He won't be interested.
He just wants to let it.
We could never get an option on a £300,000 house.
The area is too nice.
He'll probably laugh at us.
What if he is pissed off?
It's probably been let by now.
What if he credit checks us?
What if he wants references?
If he had wanted to sell it he would have put it on the market.
What's in it for him?
What if it's an agency?
What if it's a mess?
What if we couldn't let it?

What if it needs a House in Multiple Occupation licence?

What if he wants an upfront option fee that we don't have?

I could go on but does this sound familiar to you? Have you ever heard these objections before? I would love to say that I picked up the phone and dialled then and there; that would have been very brave, really masculine! Instead I put it back on the side. A week went by and it was still there.

Ben and I both worked from the third bedroom in a house we were renovating, a room that we could just about fit two small desks in. I'm not saying it was small but when we pushed our chairs back to get up from the desk they used to hit the wall behind us. Ben went downstairs to switch on the kettle so I sneaked the now crumpled piece of paper onto his desk in the hope that he would make the call. Ben suggested I call as I had more technical knowledge and could structure an argument better (and most of all because he was scared to call). I wanted Ben to call because he was more chatty and struck up relationships with people more quickly (and mainly because I was scared to call). I'm a little embarrassed that neither of us called that day or for many days thereafter. The game of sneaking the paper onto each other's desk amused us for a few days but then rather quickly became embarrassing. We didn't talk about it but I think we both felt a little ashamed that we had been putting it off.

Ben picked up the crumpled and now dusty piece of paper and said we should either call him or just chuck it out. I'm not sure how we decided but Ben agreed to call. I felt like I had both won and lost at the same time; won because Ben had agreed to call, but lost for the same reason. I didn't have time to dwell on this; Ben put Foo Fighters' "Pretender" on and turned it up loud. We always put great music on to get us in a peak state of mind before doing anything like this. Energy is everything so it's important to do anything you need to do to get yourself fired up before taking on any challenge. As soon as the track finished Ben called and then handed the phone over to me as soon as he started asking questions. This worked really well and is a model that we have continued when discussing options with landlords and letting agents.

The landlord turned out to be a solicitor and understood a bit about options (crikey, I didn't even dream up this objection when I was coming up with reasons not to call). He was struggling to understand what was in it for him and at the time I didn't know either really so I had to think on my feet. I said something about doing the maintenance so that he didn't have to worry and guaranteeing the rent. He was still unsure so I suggested putting something on an email for him. I figured that I'd buy some time whilst I thought of the benefits; we had procrastinated for over a week so another hour or so wouldn't hurt.

I started to brainstorm the benefits and was surprised to find so many; no management, no voids, no maintenance to name but a few. I put a proposal forward on email. We exchanged a few emails and calls and finally we had agreed the terms. We were in business! We had agreed our first option!

We didn't realise at the time but we were coming up with a formula for success:

1. Make contact
2. Make friends
3. Propose an option
4. Put it in writing
5. Negotiate final terms
6. Instruct the solicitors
7. Chase it until it's signed
8. Fill the property with good tenants.

There are many real life case studies in this book that show the many reasons why people would sell via lease options. Rather than reading them passively just for enjoyment I suggest you learn and write down the valuable lessons contained within each. There are many golden nuggets of information to be taken from each story.

Here are the details of the deal:

The Area

This is what Wikipedia had to say about the area:

"The area has a relatively large student population, with 21% of the over 16 population in education compared to 8.4% in Bristol and 5.1% in England and Wales.

Some of the location filming for the cult BBC sitcom The Young Ones was done in Codrington Road and elsewhere. The external shots for the famous "bank-robbing" scene in the last episode were filmed outside the now closed Bristol North Swimming Baths on Gloucester Road."

More recently Skins has been filmed in the area and it is popular with students, young professional sharers and families alike. Bishopston is one to two miles from Bristol city centre and the university. The area consists mainly of large three- to five-bedroom Victorian houses with large rooms.

The Property

The property is a large three-bedroom Victorian terrace with large rooms; downstairs there are two separate reception rooms as well as a large kitchen-breakfast room. The two reception rooms are used as bedrooms leaving a large communal kitchen and dining room.

The Situation

The landlord was a solicitor who passively invested in property using property as a place to put his surplus income rather than leaving it in the bank for a poor return . He was not investing aggressively and did not seem to have a set strategy apart from investing in good quality properties in good areas. The maintenance man showed us around the property and told us that the landlord, who no longer lived in Bristol, had bought and later sold a few properties and had in fact had this house on the market for sale a year earlier. The landlord was relatively busy with his legal practice and had previously rented the property out to students using his maintenance man to do the viewings. This year he had missed the student market. The property was a little tired (needing a new kitchen and bathroom) and was therefore less likely to attract professional sharers or a family. The property was on the market to rent for £1,000.

The Solution

We were happy to pay the £1,000 rent/lease fee as we knew we could rent out five rooms for £300 each to students therefore achieving £1,500. We proposed to buy the property in five years for a fixed price of £300,000. The seller was reluctant to fix the price so instead suggested that for every year we leased the property we would get a discount of 2.5% off the asking price for up to six years. Therefore if we leased the property for six years we would be able to buy at a 15% discount off the value at the time of purchase. Assuming a value of £350,000 the price would be £297,500, generating an equity gain of £52,500. We were potentially happy with this apart from the fact that the property needed some work. If we paid for a new kitchen and bathroom we would increase the value of the property and would therefore pay a higher price for it – effectively paying for it twice! We therefore negotiated that the seller would fit a kitchen and a bathroom at his own cost prior to the commencement of the contract.

Financial Summary

Monthly lease fee: £1,000 (Fixed for the term)
Bills: £0 (Paid by tenants)
Rent achievable: £1,500
Cash-flow: £500 per month

Purchase price: Market value at time of sale –(minus) 2.5% discount per year leased.

Term: 6 years

Summary

The most significant part of this deal is the value of the property and the amount of cash-flow achieved in relation to the investment. The property was worth £300,000 and the initial investment was just £800 (our own solicitor's fee). We had managed to secure an asset worth 375 times what we had invested! The cash-flow is £500 a month or £6,000 per year – a whopping 750% return on investment! We had our investment returned and were in profit in month two. The other important thing to note is that the landlord was not desperate in any way. This was a win-win solution suggested by the seller himself. Doing the deal was really exciting; it felt like this was what I was born to do. Doing a deal on a large property in a great area was a game changer. This gave me a paradigm shift. We had acquired this great property from a very intelligent and financially astute solicitor. The best part was that he was as happy with the deal as I was. So many property investors are looking for people who are desperate to sell and even a bit vulnerable. Don't get me wrong, it is better that people sell this way rather than get repossessed but it didn't seem completely fair as the deals seemed very one-sided. Now that I could do deals on big properties in affluent areas with no deposit and no mortgage, it felt like I had hit the jackpot! The future looked very bright.

What have you learned from this case study?

_____

_____

_____

_____

_____

_____

What key actions can you take as a result of your learning?

_____

_____

_____

_____

_____

_____

Chapter 9: Creating a Monster

One of the challenges I face is that I am always looking to the future and the next deal. Back in the real world we had seventy tenants and no systems: we had created a monster! We were warriors, great at creating business and negotiating deals, but this was a different animal that we were now dealing with. We were able to hold it off using brute force but it was tiring and took our focus away from building an empire. The problem was that neither Ben nor I were great managers/administrators. We were great at the brave stuff but management is a different skill set. The solution sounds obvious: hire a manager. The problem was that we couldn't yet afford one. The monster was growing hungry and starting to eat the cash-flow we had worked so hard to build up.

From speaking to other people, we discovered that this is one of the toughest and most common problems that businesses face. Ideally every business would start with a sales director, an operations director, a finance director and an administration assistant as well as people to do the work in the business. In practice most new start-up businesses need to keep costs to a minimum and therefore one or two end up doing everything people.

Getting Help

We knew that taking on staff, specifically someone to manage the properties and the tenants, would free up our time. We knew we could then spend our time creating new business through growing the portfolio. We had a sneaky suspicion that there would be a time delay between taking on the employee and increasing the bottom line. Managing seventy tenants was a full time job. I would love to say that we had the courage to trust in our ability and hire someone full time. Instead we dipped our toe in the water and contracted a systems specialist to help systemise our business. The first thing she did was to help us scope out all of the work that had to be done. Next she found some free property management software and began the arduous task of putting all the tenants' details on to the system. This was a time consuming process.

When the system was up and running, it really helped to organise things. It was great to have a better idea of where everything was financially. The problem was that our systems specialist wasn't cheap and rather than freeing up our time to do what we were good at she was taking up our time to help tame the monster that was our un-systemised business. This was by no means her fault. It is a natural part of the process that things get worse before they get better. This is typical whenever you get anyone to work with you because you need to invest time with them up front in order for them to help you grow your business. As well as having the extra expense, we were also having our time taken up. Also because we had only contracted her two days a week there was no time for her to do the administration that we were equally bad at. Both our time and our mind-space were still fully occupied with running a lettings business. Maybe we didn't leave it long enough but after three months it felt that we were no further forward so we decided to let her go. She was excellent value for money and she really helped implement systems that we hadn't even considered to improve the efficiency of the day-to-day work.

We didn't know if it was the right thing to do but the money was running low and we didn't want to get into trouble financially again. We knew that in many ways we were taking a step backwards. We also knew that we would need to employ someone in the future if we were to allow ourselves to reach our potential. The next step was to design things so that we would be focusing 100% on the things we were good at, in which case we would not have much to do with the property management.

Looking back I realise that I still had an employee mindset in some ways. I spent the majority of my time running the business and very little working on improving or moving the business forward and looking for more properties. A great example of this is that I used to spend the majority of the day doing maintenance and management, searching the internet for new properties whilst taking some time out to eat lunch or after I had finished working. This is when I realised I had replaced my Airbus job with just another job. I was now a property manager and maintenance guy. Deep down I knew that was crazy but the work had to be done.

A few of the properties that we had leased had been bad business decisions. We had been optimistic about the amount of money we would make because we had not taken into to account that we wouldn't have tenants 100% of the time. We also hadn't factored in much time or cost for maintenance. A couple of the properties that we had taken on only made £250 a month and we had not considered voids and maintenance. This meant that if just one room, which would rent for £350, was empty we would lose money on that entire house. This is why we had to work so hard at keeping the rooms full and also do the maintenance ourselves. We now have rules about the minimum amount of cash-flow we will make from a property, as we take into account costs associated with managing and maintaining each property.

Chapter 10: The Guest House – Option Deal Two

Between the stresses of doing a bad job managing a portfolio and maintaining properties, I had come across another property that would make a great student house. Now I just had to persuade the owner of the benefits of a lease option. The property was for sale with two agents, which is great as both agents want the business. If one agent sells the property, the one that doesn't make the sale doesn't make any money. This means each agent is a bit more motivated. One of the agents was a big chain and the other a small independent. I felt the small agent would be hungrier and that the larger one would have to explain the concept to their area manager. I called the smaller agent, to whom, incidentally, I had previously explained lease options. I think he half-understood the concept at the time and was willing to put the offer forward. The property looked pretty old from the outside and we jokingly called it the ghost house. We followed the same process that had worked before:

- Make contact
- Build rapport/relationship

- View property
- Research the area and the numbers
- Put offer forward in writing and explain (ideally in person)
- Negotiate
- Sign contracts
- Refurbish (if required)
- Fill with students or professionals.

Case Study: Clift House Road

The Area

Southville is an area one to one-and-a-half miles from Bristol's city centre. Its locality makes it very popular with professional sharers and students alike. Southville also has a wide range of bars, restaurants and coffee shops that are popular with young professionals.

The House

Clift House Road is a seven-bedroom ex–guest house with all rooms en suite. The owner had bought it with her partner for £250,000 in 2007 and lovingly renovated the property to run it as a lifestyle business.

The Situation

Unfortunately the owner split up with her partner and was unable to sell the property so she had rented it out to students. The students didn't look after the property and left early, leaving the owner to pay the monthly mortgage payments of £1,500. These mortgage payments were crippling and so the seller put the property up for sale again at £360,000. With no sale after two months the seller reduced the price to £330,000 but the property still didn't sell. This was probably because in 2010 investors required 35% deposits for Houses of Multiple Occupation.

The Numbers an Investor Would Need to Know:

Deposit £112,000 (35% * £330,000)
Stamp duty £9,900 (£330,000 * 3%)
House of Multiple Occupation Licence and work required £10,000
Legal fees £2,000
Total £133,900

Close to £135,000 is a large upfront investment for a single property in a recession. It is clear to see how even a potentially great cash-flowing property like this was not selling.

The Solution

As investors who specialise in large multi-let properties, we knew that we could rent out each room for £380 a month including bills. This means that the total revenue from the house would be £2,660 per month. We also knew that this property was in a great area for students. Students are council tax exempt, which means that the total cost for utilities would be near £250 per month. With this in mind we were able to lease the property for £1,500 a month covering the monthly mortgage costs. We also agreed to pay the maintenance costs as part of the deal. We set up a five-year lease with the exclusive option to purchase the property at any time within the lease period.

Summary of the Deal

Term: 5 years
Purchase price: £330,000
Monthly lease fee: £1,500
Utility bills: around £250
Maintenance: paid by leaseholder
Insurance: paid by leaseholder
Rental income: £2,660 (£380 * 7 bedrooms)
Profit: £900 per month

Win-Win

The case study above demonstrates how lease options can be used to create great win-win solutions. The owner was able to relieve her financial burden very quickly and achieve full market value for her property (£330,000). Lease option contracts can be written in weeks rather than traditional sales, which take three to six months to complete.

This was another great deal; we had secured a great property for less than £10,000 and it would make more than that every year in cash-flow! The £10,000 investment included the agent's fee, the solicitor's fee and the money to get the HMO licence. This property stretched us because we had to borrow the money from an investor, which we hadn't done before. This was a great deal as I was easily able to demonstrate our ability to repay the money and also to secure the loan against the £30,000 equity in my flats.

What have you learned from this case study?

_____

_____

_____

_____

_____

_____

What key actions can you take as a result of your learning?

_____

_____

_____

_____

_____

_____

Chapter 11: Kingswood – The Expensive Option

Whilst negotiating on the guest house we were also in negotiation on a property slightly out of town. At the time the Local Housing Allowance for a five-bedroom house was £1,300 per month. We had been contacted by a letting agent from whom we had previously leased two properties. One of her landlords had a property that had had a string of bad tenants and he was fed up. We viewed the property and decided that we would only lease it if we had the option to purchase. Having the option to purchase gave us more control and would mean that any improvements made to the property would benefit us when we bought it. The property was out of town and we didn't want to rent out the rooms, because this far from the centre of town rooms would be less desirable. It would also take more time to rent them out.

This deal would only work if we could lease the property from the landlord for significantly less than we could rent it to a family. The Local Housing Allowance rate paid by the council was £1,300 and this meant we could make a margin by leasing the property from the owner for less than this, then renting it out to council tenants. We felt that renting to a family would be stress-free compared to dealing with our usual five tenancies per property. The landlord was keen to get the market rent of £900 for this property. Because we knew the council would pay £1,300 and also because it was possible to get the council to pay us directly, we were happy to pay this to achieve a £400 profit. Unfortunately, neither Ben nor I had rented to council tenants before and our inexperience proved costly. Our tenants moved in with rent and deposit and with the understanding that the council would pay us directly. As soon as we had signed the agreement, the Government's rules changed and the rate for five-bedroom properties was scrapped, meaning that the most any tenant could claim by would be the four-bedroom rate of £900. One of our tenants then got a job and this immediately reduced the amount they were able to claim in benefits. The tenants were then responsible for paying the difference to us, which did not happen despite continual promises to catch up on the rent. It took seven months to get rid of these tenants, and cost a total of £7,000. Looking back, it is clear we had moved away from what we knew and had become good at. We had also rather foolishly based our decision to take the option relying on the Government's benefits policy rather than on what we could rent it for privately. Governments can change policy at any time so I think it is unwise to base decisions on this with no 'Plan B'.

What have you learned from this case study?

_____

_____

_____

_____

_____

_____

What key actions can you take as a result of your learning?

_____

_____

_____

_____

_____

_____

Chapter 12: Getting a Coach

Desperate to grow as people as well as a business, we toyed with the idea of getting a coach. We knew deep down that although we had already achieved a lot we were capable of so much more. I feel that the majority of people only operate at about 10-20% of their potential. I didn't want to be one of those people. It was great that we were beginning to secure lease option deals, meaning that as well as generating short term cash-flow from renting out the property room by room, we were also securing the option to buy the properties at a fixed price at any time during the five- to seven-year option period. This meant that we would also profit from the capital appreciation (property value increase). The problem was we were not doing enough of this.

A lot of people turn their noses up at the idea of being coached/mentored; they have the impression that you only get coached if you are not any good. This couldn't be further from the truth! Every champion has a great coach. Take the England rugby team as an example. In the run up to the World Cup in 2003 they were winning all of their games, Clive Woodward the manager employed a coach for the forwards, a coach for the backs, a scrummaging coach, a coach who specialised only in peripheral vision, a nutritionist, fitness coaches and physiotherapists. He even took the team on marine training. Did he do this because they were no good? No, he did it because he wanted them to be the best. I highly recommend Clive Woodward's book "Winning".

With this in mind we approached someone who we knew to be great at systems and management, our greatest weakness. We didn't have a clue what he would charge or even if he would be interested in working with us. We came off the phone buzzing and sure he would take us to the next level. It was only an initial call to see if we could potentially work together. Unfortunately, our coach-to-be started to have some problems at home and decided that it wouldn't be right to take on new clients at that time.

We were back to square one, and then Ben asked a great question. If you could have any coach who would it be? *"Simon Zutshi"* was my reply, quickly followed by *"but he doesn't do private coaching"*. Anyone who knows Ben will know how cheeky he can be and he suggested that we call Simon and ask him. Surely we couldn't afford him. The truth was that we couldn't afford not to have him coach us. That said, paying out a lot of money on a monthly basis would soon sink us if we didn't increase the bottom line by at least the same amount. The first thing that Simon did was to get us to double the amount that we were charging for mentoring (we were helping clients increase monthly cash-flow by hundreds, even thousands of pounds per month and only charging a pittance for it). As we mentor a couple of people per month this really helped us pay for him. The next thing he suggested was not as popular; despite the fact that we had really stretched ourselves to afford him, he wanted us to take on an employee. Initially we pushed back at the idea; we had no idea how we would afford it and yet we knew it was the only way to really move forward. We were once again in the chicken and egg situation. We needed the employee to allow us to focus on our strengths to make more money but we needed more money to pay the employee.

Chapter 13: Help ... We Need a Female!

One day whilst I was away mentoring, Ben reached the end of his tether dealing with tenants and management. That morning his girlfriend told us we needed a woman to sort us out. The Gumtree advertisement title he wrote read: "*Help ... We need a female administration assistant.*" Ben was never afraid to take action. The first I heard about this advert was the next day, when Ben was out mentoring and I was in the office receiving strange calls from people needing a job. The first was from a young lad who asked if he could apply despite not being female because he had some experience, I set up an interview for Monday. The next call was from a girl called Tanya. She asked what the job involved, I shrugged my shoulders (that doesn't work so well on the phone by the way). I may or may not have answered. The next question was "*Are you in the office for the next half an hour and can I pop my CV in?*" She was keen! This was a good sign!

She turned up twenty-five minutes later with a CV in hand, still a bit dazed and confused and not exactly sure what job she was there for, I thought maybe I should ask her some questions ... No, she didn't want a cup of tea. Damn, I was all out of questions! Luckily she had a few of her own. What was involved in the job? There was no real description on the advert, apparently. Ben never was one for detail. I couldn't really answer all her questions specifically but I was able to tell her the general things that we needed help with. I think she was glad to see that whilst most people were moaning about the recession we were out making things happen! Tanya was very keen to work with us and was asking whether it would be possible to develop it into a full time role if she helped us to grow the business. Tanya had run a property business in Bulgaria renovating houses and selling to overseas buyers. Her business became more challenging as the financial markets stopped lending to overseas investors. So she had some worthwhile experience but none in lettings. I wasn't really concerned as attitude is what is important to me. I wanted to hire her and just had to check it out with Ben.

Ben had interviewed someone who had lettings experience and we agreed to both interview each other's candidates. Jen, the girl Ben had found, had the right experience and could have got on with the job quickly. She was very nice and friendly but just looking for a job part time whilst at university. It was also just a job and there was no enthusiasm coming from her. She was studying architecture and felt the job was below her. In my opinion Tanya was head and shoulders above her.

Ben interviewed Tanya and initially there was no rapport between them whatsoever. Ben is very chatty and Tanya, being new to England and lacking in confidence about her spoken English, was a little abrupt. Ben saw both sides; he wanted someone friendly, but also knew that a person with drive would be good for the business. The other good thing we noticed was that she wasn't afraid to tell us off for not being organised. This attitude would work well when dealing with tenants. Still unsure we called Ben's girlfriend, Kerry, who is great with people and had recently recruited staff. She agreed that we needed someone with drive who wouldn't mind kicking our tenants arses (or ours actually). Ben and I had always been quite casual with tenants and had then got annoyed when they were casual about paying the rent on time. Neither Ben nor I ever wanted to be the kind of people to tell tenants off but this was exactly what some of them needed. Needless to say we were happy to gradually hand over the reins.

Chapter 14: Getting Perspective

As we started to put systems in place and to look more closely at the numbers we realised that some of the properties didn't work as well as we would like financially. These also happened to be the properties that gave us the most hassle. Long term we knew they would have to go. Now that we were employing someone to manage them, the profit was reduced due to the wage that we apportioned between the properties.

A couple of the properties were making so little money that a two-week void/vacancy would be enough to wipe out that whole property's profit for a month. We had been over optimistic and had not accounted for any void periods when doing our initial figures. Many landlords wrongly assume 100% occupancy and 100% payment. This we now realised was very short sighted. We had been kidding ourselves that the properties were making more money than they were. We could only kid ourselves for so long. The evidence was clear – although we were financially free and didn't have to go to work, there was never a big surplus in our bank account. Now we knew that we had to get rid of these properties but there was a problem. We had taken on a property manager based on the income of these properties. If we were going to get rid of some of the properties, how would we afford a property manager? Our mentor convinced us that we would make more money if we kept the manager and focused on finding more deals. All we needed to do was to endure the short term pain to allow us to grow in the near future. Within a few months of taking Tanya on we had replaced the cash-flow from the poorly performing properties and also provided enough to cover Tanya's cost. The only bad thing was that Simon our mentor was right AGAIN!

Chapter 15: My Public Speaking Rollercoaster

I have always been keen to share knowledge and the idea of inspiring others really ignites me. It would seem natural then that I should share my knowledge on stage to inspire as many people as possible. This all seems logical, yes? The problem is that phobias don't follow logic. I had a massive fear of public speaking. My first and worst approach was to just ignore it and hope it would go away. Ben and I were asked to share our successes at the London and Birmingham Property Investors Network (PIN) meeting for just ten minutes as part of a presentation about Simon Zutshi's Mastermind programme. Birmingham was the first meeting and I had to speak for just five minutes. I prepared five or six slides and because I was petrified about presenting I just avoided the problem. I didn't practice the presentation as I didn't even want to think about it.

It was the big night. Ben and I were clapped on to the stage − they obviously didn't know how bad I was going to be. Ben spoke for the first five minutes, anyone who knows Ben knows that he is naturally gifted at presenting. The problem was that this made it worse for me; he was doing really well and getting lots of laughs and the pressure was mounting.

I started to speak and my voice was shaky, I felt the first bead of sweat build on my forehead, the first of many. I noticed that I was rocking from one foot to the other. I have since learned that people rock (mainly mentally ill people) as it gives a sense of comfort akin to being rocked as a baby. As I was rocking I was moving backwards slightly with every step, by the end of the presentation I was backed against a wall slightly behind one of the Mastermind promotional banners. I remember nothing about the presentation content except for the last slide. Having read loads of inspiring books, at this point I wanted to share the most amazing quote:

"It is not the critic who counts; not the man who points out how the strong man stumbles, or where the doer of deeds could have done them better. The credit belongs to the man who is actually in the arena, whose face is marred by dust and sweat and blood; who strives valiantly; who errs, who comes short again and again, because there is no effort without error and shortcoming; but who does actually strive to do the deeds; who knows great enthusiasms, the great devotions; who spends himself in a worthy cause; who at the best knows in the end the triumph of high achievement, and who at the worst, if he fails, at least fails while daring greatly, so that his

place shall never be with those cold and timid souls who neither know victory nor defeat".

Theodor Roosevelt

Needless to say I didn't do this speech justice. As I stood there I was taken back to a time when I was about six or seven years old, a little boy who at the time was very poor at reading, made to read in front of the class. My worst nightmare.

People still clapped as we left the stage, maybe more in sympathy than anything else! When you give a talk and are evidently nervous, afterwards people usually say *"Oh no, we couldn't tell at all"*. After this speech someone said *"Well, at least you did it"*. When someone says that, you know it must have been bad.

A week or two later I was due to speak in London, an equally large meeting with ninety to one hundred people. What should I do? Let Ben do it alone? He was more than capable. It wasn't that I didn't want to make a fool of myself again; I have a very high pain threshold so that wasn't a problem. I thought more about Simon's brand and about the audience; nobody wants to see somebody die on stage. Ben, supportive as ever, was happy to do it alone but thought I should push through the fear. I wanted a second opinion so I called Simon; Simon said it was completely up to me but that I deserved to be up there as we had been so successful. I didn't deliberate long, in the words of Richard Branson, *"Screw it, let's do it"*.

I don't remember if I rehearsed much, if at all, before London; I'm not sure if the penny had dropped at the time, that this was part of the problem. London, however, was a lot better. I was still nervous but planted my feet to the floor so I didn't rock, and dropped the reading of the long quote. It must have been a lot better as I ended up on a date with someone from the audience!

It was a little while before we got the opportunity to speak again and when we did I was again in two minds. On the one hand I have always believed that you should play to your strengths, Ben is a great public speaker and so I didn't really need to do it. On the other hand one of my biggest goals/values is to inspire others. I was told by many people that if I just practiced and kept getting up on stage that I would get better and better. What I really wanted was a cast iron guarantee that this was the case. I would definitely have been willing to go through all the effort if I knew for sure I would be successful, but then life is not like that, is it? You have to just work hard and have faith that it will work out for the best. Life would be easy if you knew what the outcome would be, but it would be a lot less enjoyable and rewarding. Luckily for me, and for the thousands of people I have now spoken in front of, the desire to inspire was triumphant and I regularly share my experiences and knowledge from stage. The results of facing my fear have been holistic, not only has my confidence grown on stage but in many other areas of business too.

Getting Published

I have always been a great fan of 'Your Property Network' magazine. Ant Lyons and the guys do a great job of continually producing new and relevant content. Like many readers I find the case studies to be the most enjoyable part as I find it really interesting to see what other successful people are doing. As you can imagine I was really chuffed when I was given the chance to write an article. Ant wanted me to share my experience of using options to secure large, high value properties in desirable areas.

At the time the few investors using option contracts were finding sellers in negative equity with no choice but to sell this way. I used the opportunity to show how options could be used at the top end of the market because they are so win-win. I was delighted and proud to see the four-page spread. It was a great opportunity to look back to see how far I had come. Just two years earlier I had been sacked from my job and had cash-flow of -£50 (minus).

Please visit my website to see a copy of the article www.barrydaviesproperty.com.

Chapter 16: Starting to Help Others

Having replaced our 'employee' income relatively quickly people were interested to learn how we had done so and, more importantly, whether we could help them to do the same. I first met Divian when I spoke at the Birmingham pin meeting that very first time. I think that was his first property meeting, he was young and very keen to get started in property. At the time I was selling another landlord's portfolio using lease options. The landlord was in negative equity and was now making more money out of his profession as a dentist and wanted to walk away from his properties. This landlord had bought his properties back in 2005-2007 when property investing was fashionable and everyone wanted to be a property investor, seeing it as a way to get rich quick. Needless to say property lost its sparkle for most when the market crashed.

I met Divian the week following the pin meeting as he was interested in buying the option deals. Divian decided to invest in his education instead of the deals which was a wise choice. He was interested in our leasing strategy, but we had no training service because at that time we were not confident enough about our ability to mentor others. We did go on to help him later as our own confidence grew.

Mentoring Case Studies

All of the case studies are written first hand by the people who have done the deals. I feel it is important to leave them unedited, because I want to present their stories as they stand, rather than play around with them to say what I want. I have simply asked them to include their history, details of their deal(s), the motivation of the seller, what made them successful and what they are up to now. Another reason for leaving them untouched is that they are such amazing stories; they are both informative and inspiring. I hope you enjoy them as much as I have.

Divian's Story

I am twenty-three years old, almost twenty-four and I started my property journey two years ago. At this point of time I had been out of University for about two years and was working in Subway making sandwiches, I had been promoted from sandwich artist to supervisor. I had previously applied to over one hundred investment banks to no avail as I had graduated into the recession. After many months looking for other jobs after the investment banking jobs, and being rejected, I decided I was fed up and wanted to run my own business, go straight to what I wanted (I had wanted to run my own business and run a few small businesses since the age of fourteen; and had wanted to invest in property since the age of sixteen or seventeen). I almost had a chance to buy the Subway franchise branch that I worked at, although the business went bankrupt before I could move on it. Before this bankruptcy my boss told me that I should go into property and I didn't need a load of money to do so. After an hour long discussion I decided to go home and investigate. To my surprise I found forums, mailing lists and other information on this new world of investment, which opened up possibilities to me that I had never thought would be possible.

I decided to invest in my education and went on a few different courses, the biggest one took me a year to complete and I had to borrow about £8,000 from my parents and grandparents to go on it. This is where I hit the BIG dilemma. My dad told me he was lending me this money on the condition I didn't borrow ANY money from ANYONE in the family. I am twenty-two years old, all my mates are at university or have graduated and none of them had money! The ONLY people with money were my family, but I couldn't borrow from them. Now I have learned some real creative ways of buying property, however they all require some level of money, not much but something. I went through this course and made a lot of friends, took HUGE action with no avail. Now I knew I was going to be successful it was a given in my mind, I just needed to persist and find the right way of achieving it for me which is when I met two guys – Ben and Barry.

Ben and Barry – these guys taught me a way of buying property, supported me, coached me and were here every step of the way in making the deals happen. The best tool they gave me was to come to my house, work on my area and make the calls on the day to view houses and actually secure the deals. None of the previous stuff of sitting in a room getting hyped and then waking up in the morning and losing all motivation. This was learn it, simulate it, do it, improve, do it again, improve, do it again and continue to do it until you mastered it.

This is where my journey really began, to date I have a share in five properties, which have been acquired within six months, all bar one (as we literally just bought it at the time of writing this) are making me money. I am months away from quitting my job, and to be honest it is only because I committed to working six months more in this job that it will be six months. I won't need this job in three months' time.

The deals I picked up have varied. We have bought some outright and lease optioned others. The best ones are lease options; my best property has figures as per below:

3–bedroom, 2-reception room, mid terrace in Leicester
Initial investment (including first month's rent, furniture, etc) = £1,500
Monthly lease fee = £575pcm
Bills = £350pcm
Total monthly cost = £925pcm

Monthly rental income = £1,375pcm
Monthly profit = £1,375 - £925 = £450pcm

All that profit on a property I don't even own!

The landlord was simply fed up, he had got control of the property from his sister-in-law who was too old to look after it herself and so she gave him the keys to do something and look after the house. He rented it to some immigrants and they were nice people and he was earning £600pcm from it. So why would he give it to me? Well I offered him £575 guaranteed rent regardless of void periods, look after the property in terms of maintenance and all he had to do is look after the boiler and the structure of the property. So in actual fact he now makes more money from it.

The thing I saw in the property is that both of these reception rooms were actual rooms sectioned off. So this three-bed turned into four double rooms and a box room which gives a very high return. I make a 137% return on my money just in the first year and I have signed a three-year lease.

I made this win-win as the landlord got a lower rent but also lower maintenance/void periods; the landlord also doesn't have tenants to deal with and he is a busy guy working full time. I got the fact that I could use my skill in finding tenants and employing the multi-letting strategy to maximize the rent on this property without taking too much risk.

I would say there are a few things that make me successful; however the top traits I have are persistence, consistency in action, fearlessness and openness/willingness to change.

Persistence – to have the drive to keep going no matter what until you get your desired result.

Consistency – to ensure you do the small little thing every day, like make five calls a day no matter what, even if I had to walk the streets to find phone numbers I was prepared to do this (luckily I didn't have to).

Fearlessness – the ability to be 100% present in the moment and just think about the task you are dealing with, and worry about the things that are going to go wrong when they occur because 99 times out for 100 the things that go wrong are the things you never even knew could go wrong.

Openness/willingness to change – Albert Einstein says *"the definition of someone who is mad is someone who continues to do the same thing over and over and expects different results"*. I was open to suggestion and I had a willingness to learn from my mistakes and try different methods of talking to people.

Now that I have agents working for me, the days of calling around to get people to give me properties have died down a little; now I receive the phone calls and I call the shots. I also have people working for me to find tenants and look after my current tenants. The beautiful thing about this is that I focus on the bit I LOVE and I am great at. I wouldn't say I am a master; however I am on the road to getting there.

What this has allowed to me do is go and coach people on how to become successful and they have had fantastic results, their life is more fulfilling and they feel driven to achieve as well as try new things in life. This is my way of giving back and I have a mission to change the life of every single human being I meet, as well as proceeding on my path to financial empowerment in my life, as I have chosen this possibility! Watch out Richard Branson, here I come!

Divian Mistry

My Observations and Comments on Divian

I met Divian at the beginning of his journey into property investing and self-development and it has been a pleasure to watch him grow into the superstar he's becoming. Divian very much reminded me of my journey into property – loads of action and no massive results to speak of for the first few months. From the outside it was clear to see that he was just on the cusp of success and that it would come if he just kept going. It was great to have the opportunity to work with Divian to help him through this stage of his development.

Lots of people who invest in training and education are looking for the secret ingredient, or the magic pill that rockets them to success. Divian knows more than anyone that there is no magic pill. We helped Divian to consistently take the action required to become successful and we were there to support and inspire him to just keep going until the results came, which they surely did.

These days I don't hear from Divian much at all, occasionally I get a phone call with a quick question and then he's off again onto the next deal. That first deal seemed to give Divian the belief and the confidence he required to get him going; now he has so much momentum that there is no stopping him.

What have you learned from this case study?

_____

_____

_____

_____

_____

_____

What key actions can you take as a result of your learning?

_____

_____

_____

_____

_____

_____

Chapter 17: Helping an Old Friend - Matt's Case Study

Whilst travelling around the country speaking at property networking events, we decided to stay at Ben's friend's house rather than travel back to Bristol. This is where Matt's property story began. This is what happened in Matt's own words.

Matt's Story

My wife and I had been talking about investing in property since 2009, but we never did anything about it. I am a Chartered Engineer and my wife is a Commercial Marketing Manager. We both work for big blue chip companies and work long hours. We knew nothing about property or investing. We own our property but realised how little control we actually had over that deal.

We were under the impression that the only way to buy property was the 'traditional' approach of saving the deposit, getting a mortgage and putting an offer in. We had no idea about any other methods or strategies for investing in property. We wanted to start investing but didn't know how to take the first step.

It was at this point that we contacted Ben and Barry at Smart Property Investment; the directors of the company were friends of ours. I had met Ben at university in 2002. They recommended we read Property Magic by Simon Zutshi. This book opened our eyes to strategies and techniques for investing in property that we had never thought of. We were really inspired by this book and the discussions I had been having with Barry. With these new tools at our disposal we were ready to start investing in property.

We didn't do anything immediately. There didn't seem to be enough time with work and other commitments. We had identified a potential lease option deal on a property that was on the same street that we lived on, but didn't do anything about it. We talked about the deal for hours on end but never acted. What was holding us back? It was in March 2011, about six months after identifying the deal that I plucked up the courage and knocked on the door. The property had been on the market for around twelve months. I knew the seller of the property a little, but I didn't even know his name. I introduced myself formally and told him I was interested in taking his property off his hands. He invited me in to look around. I asked him some questions about the property and about his situation. He was recently divorced. He wanted to sell the property so he could move in with his new partner. He was self-employed and work was hard to come by at this time so he was struggling to pay the mortgage and had arrears on the property.

He had re-mortgaged a couple of years before and so there was not much equity in the property. He realised that he would probably lose money while selling the property and he was happy to take this hit. As there was not much equity, a below market value purchase of the property seemed unlikely.

I told him I would like to rent the property from him over a long period. I explained that during this time I would be fully responsible for the property and would pay his mortgage. I then said that during the lease period I would purchase the property from him at a value we agree today. He had never heard of this before and at first he was sceptical. He asked if this was legal. I assured him it was and told him I would review the figures and get back to him before he made any firm decision.

Due to the fact that he had re-mortgaged, the monthly mortgage payments were high at around £530 per month. I did a bit of research and decided that we would rent the property for around £600 per month. This meant the cash-flow on the property was only £70 per calendar month. We almost walked away from this deal but because it was our first we were reluctant to do so as we knew the house was in good condition and in a good area. The property was valued at £110,000 and because we were not getting a high monthly cash-flow I explained to the seller that we would need to secure some of the property's equity. We made an offer to cover his mortgage and have the option to buy the property within a five-year period for £85,000 which secured £25,000 of equity for ourselves. At first he seemed reluctant but after some discussion he could see the benefits. He would not have to pay any fees and the deal would be done in around four weeks meaning he would not have to make any more mortgage payments. He could move straight out and get on with his life. He gratefully accepted the offer. It was at this point that we realised how little we knew about lease options. We contacted Barry at Smart Property Investment and with his help and support we sealed the deal. The seller was so happy he gave us the keys before the deal was complete. We tidied the property with a few coats of paint and got it on the rental market and found a tenant before the deal was complete. The day the deal completed we moved our tenant in, it seemed so surreal to have achieved so much as novices but we did. The amount of time we invested in total was around twenty hours. Half of a normal working week and we invested approximately £1,000 pounds into the deal.

The hardest thing about securing this deal was the first step. It seemed so scary and risky. It was much easier to make excuses such as 'the cash-flow is too low' or 'we haven't got the time'. In reality we made £25,000 in twenty hours and that is not taking into consideration the monthly cash-flow or capital growth. We essentially stalled on this deal for six months and were fortunate that another investor didn't find this deal. Once the first step was made it was really simple.

Since then we have secured two more property deals in 2011. We are quite proud to have secured three properties in nine months whilst holding down full time jobs without any specialist knowledge of investing. We are still learning but are looking forward to finding and investing in more properties in 2012. It's going to be another successful year.

Matthew Gavin

My Observations and Comments

Matt has written a rather formal account of our meeting as I guess he thought he should make us sound professional. Matt is Ben's best mate from university who was more used to drinking with Ben than having any real business relationship. Matt was interested in property but didn't know how to get started. We went to Matt and Fiona's for dinner and stayed overnight on our way to work with one of our clients. Matt and Fiona were both interested in what we had been doing in property and we talked over taking options on property whilst we tucked into our pizza. Matt mentioned that a property just up the road had been on the market for at least six months. Then he quickly added that he couldn't easily rent a house out where they lived because they don't come up for rent often.

Has this ever happened to you? Do you come up with a great idea then quickly find reasons not to act because it's uncomfortable to proceed with the idea? This is called procrastination!

Ben is very intuitive and can smell procrastination a mile off and called Matt's bluff. Within three minutes there was an advert for Matt's property for rent on Gumtree.com (the free classified advert site). Within ten minutes the phone rang ... It couldn't be? It was! That was the first of three or four enquiries within twenty-four hours (before Matt removed the advert to get some peace). That first phone call seemed to have a profound effect on Matt and Fiona. They had decided there were no tenants and then their belief had been blown out of the water. Where did that unfounded belief come from?

More importantly what other stories had they been telling themselves that might not be true? They realised that day that they were getting in their own way and making assumptions that were holding them back.

Matt and Fiona really took the bull by the horns and decided to go for this property. Matt had no formal training at this point but was a fast learner so we sent him on a mission to approach the vendor and find out what his situation was. With some further coaching Matt sealed the deal. I think this case study shows how simple things can be. So many investors think they need to know everything before they do a deal. Matt proved that deals can be rather simple if you just ask the right questions. Maybe it was a blessing in disguise that Matt had little experience – nobody had told him that he couldn't just take options on property and make money out of it without owning it, so he just did it.

Matt and Fiona have now undergone further training and are off to a flying start in their property career having secured two other deals since this one. What a great year!

Matt was able to secure this property for a price below what it was worth and below what was owing on the mortgage at the time, because it is a repayment mortgage. Matt is therefore paying the mortgage off during the next five years. The down side to this is that the property won't make much money over the short term. The great thing is that they are building a nice pot of money due to the mortgage capital being paid off over the five year term. This deal might not work for everyone due to the small monthly cash-flow but Matt and Fiona have good jobs so the long term equity is great for them

What have you learned from this case study?

_____

_____

_____

_____

_____

_____

What key actions can you take as a result of your learning?

_____

_____

_____

_____

_____

_____

Progression of our Mentoring

Sharing our knowledge from the stage at Simon's Mastermind programme and on the PIN circuit really began to get people talking. Making thousands of pounds cash-flow on properties you don't own, have no mortgage for and haven't paid deposits on was big news. As a result many people wanted to learn how and the popularity of the mentoring grew; as these people started to get results interest really started to increase.

We still offer mentoring on a limited basis. If you would like to know more, please email barry@barrydaviesproperty.co.uk.

Chapter 18: Dillon's Case Study

Dillon was a pleasure to work with. We usually select clients who have a bit more property experience under their belts, but were convinced by Dillon's charm and confidence. Dillon had read a couple of books and attended a one day seminar. That was the sum of his property knowledge. He had substantial business and consulting knowledge, and people experience; additionally, he was professional and well presented.

Before the on-site part of the mentoring, we do a lot of preparatory work with the client over the phone and internet to research their area. During this work we discovered a property that was advertised with discounted rent for the first few months. We know a lot of landlords and not many of them give much away for free. There had to be a catch, or as trained eyes would see it, an opportunity. Dillon bravely spoke to the seller and viewed the property. Here is his story.

Dillon's Story: the Background

Sourced via Rightmove.

Property marketed for rent, at a reduced price (from £595 to £545) due to 'work needed'.

On viewing, 'work needed' translated to 'total refurbishment required'.

Negotiation

All negotiation had to be done by telephone as the owners had already moved out of the country. This was an investment property that clearly wasn't even paying for itself, never mind making them any money so I felt that a mid- to long-term managed lease with option to buy would work well for us all; especially as they were out of the country.

Key learning point: when Barry says *"Make sure you know who the real decision maker is,"* he means it! Having had Heads of Terms signed remarkably quickly with the person named on the mortgage agreement, I received a call from a very irate husband accusing me of trying to rip his wife off and *"make a quick buck"* out of her.

The upshot was that some very genuine negotiation and tactful education needed to take place before a second set of Heads of Terms could be forwarded on to the solicitor.

We came to a mutually agreeable package which wasn't a million miles away from the original deal but that ensured both stakeholders were (a) fully bought in, (b) 100% supportive of my plans for the property and (c) pleased to be entering what essentially amounted to a joint venture deal.

I was already planning the works and visualising a house full of tenants when the solicitor telephoned me to say that the other party were being advised NOT to enter the deal. Their solicitor's reasoning was that lease options are a rip off and the property would be lost through mortgage arrears. His lack of understanding of lease options, and this deal in particular, shone through since I had never actually agreed to pay the mortgage directly. Nonetheless, this was a critical sticking point that had to be resolved. Having educated an irate husband, I now entered into battle with an inept solicitor whose interpretation of "protect and serve" could very nearly scupper a true win-win deal. After all, no one else in their right mind would have taken this property on.

Having successfully jumped through a few more flaming rings of fire, the result was:

Lease price: £1
Lease period: 6 years.

Lease fee: £495
Purchase Price: £115,000
Cost of renovation: £10,000
Legal fees: £800 + £800 (mine plus theirs)

TOTAL: £11,601

Income:

3 doubles @ £75 per week = £225 per week
2 singles @ £65 per week = £130 per week

Annualised monthly income: £1,538.33

Outgoings:

Lease fee @ £495
Bills @ £500 (gas and council tax are by far the biggest outgoings)

Monthly Total: £995

Positive cash-flow: £543.33

Annualised gross income: £6,519.96
Payback period of £11,601: 22 months.

Dillon

My Observations and Comments

Dillon jumped through a lot of hoops with this property and showed great tenacity. The key learning here is that Dillon had built a great relationship with the seller. This relationship along with Dillon's great negotiating kept the deal on track. One particular hurdle was that the sellers insisted on using their own solicitor. This can be a challenge if the solicitor isn't open minded. When creating a great win-win solution, these challenges can be overcome because both sides really want the deal to happen. Many investors and trainers preach that you should insist on the seller using a solicitor that you select. Following this strategy would have killed this deal plus many of the deals that I've done where the seller insists on using their own solicitor. I am happy to proceed with the sellers using their own solicitor so that they are comfortable; however, I now insist that they pay their own fees.

Dillon has since gone on to buy another HMO using joint venture partners. He has a great go-getter attitude, which is key to his success. I look forward to hearing about Dillon's next deal.

What have you learned from this case study?

_____

_____

_____

_____

_____

_____

What key actions can you take as a result of your learning?

_____

_____

_____

_____

_____

_____

Chapter 19: Clifton Wood – Moving Up in the World!

Many of the challenges that I have written about happened years ago, but the challenges don't stop. We still face challenges all of the time. Every time we step up to the next level. First we bought our first investment, then another, and then our first multi-let. Later we became comfortable with that and did some more deals. Now it was time to step up to the next level again, a four-storey townhouse needing complete renovation had become available. It was available to cash buyers only as there were holes in the roof, a tree growing out of the basement and some other structural issues. These problems were the least of our worries though. I had been to view the property and knew we could tackle the work required. I even figured that doing the work would be an advantage because we could improve the layout significantly. If someone was going to buy this place for cash they would be making a seriously low offer. I knew that by using options I wouldn't need to pay for the property and would only need to find funds for the refurbishment. This meant I would be able to pay more than a cash buyer. I had written a proposal that even I was impressed with. We drove to the estate agents and were walking from the car to the front door. Four feet away from the door I froze; this was one of the most upmarket estate agents in town. These people were looking for someone with £350,000 cash, and here I was about to offer them a pound. Who was I kidding? They wouldn't buy this idea. They would surely laugh at us. These people were so posh they were from up-town Bristol and didn't even sound like farmers! Ben looked back at me. *"Come on"* he said. *"What am I going to say?"* I said. We just stood there for a few seconds, there was nothing I could say to dress up the fact that I wasn't offering to buy it just yet. I quickly thought about how Branson or Trump would handle it. They would confidently walk in there knowing that this was the best solution. That's what we did. When we went in we sat in front of the chap who had shown us the property (we had good experience of dealing with a hungry youngish agent before). We began to explain our proposal and the manager quickly ushered the young chap out of the way so that he could talk to us. It took some time to get the idea across; as with most agents, this was the first he had heard of this idea. In the end he was happy to put it forward and even recommend that the owner accept the offer, as we were offering more than anyone else.

The owner was more stuck in his ways and after a lot of deliberation decided against the idea of selling using a lease option. On the face of it this was a defeat. We were however victorious over our fear. We didn't get the deal but we had stepped up and faced our fear. Our reward was much greater confidence! Oh, and we did a much better deal on the house five doors down the street a few weeks later!

Whenever you grow as a business or as a person there will be challenges, and as crazy as it sounds that's why high achievers do it. High achievers love to stretch themselves even though it means discomfort initially. This is because the feeling of achievement is so powerful. Without growth there is no point in living and I am a great believer in the philosophy that states that if you are not growing, you are dying. This is why I will never stop. I will continue to challenge myself as long as I live. Is it greed? No, it's cool having good stuff but its only stuff. It is the desire to always do better. Probably the most common cause of failure is a lack of purpose and lack of progress. Despite not getting the above-mentioned property, whilst on a second viewing we spotted another house up for sale in the same street. What's more, this was also in need of work and was with an agent with whom we had done options before.

The following is a case study which has been included to show how it is possible to move into a great area without having to put a massive deposit into a property.

This is definitely a perk of the job for any investor using options. This case study also shows how it is possible to use options to secure high value properties from people who are not desperate to sell.

Case Study: Clifton Wood

The Area

Bellevue Crescent is a true crescent of beautiful four-storey town houses in Clifton Wood, one of the most desirable areas of Bristol. It is a ten-minute walk from the city centre, ten minutes from Clifton Village and just five minutes from the waterfront area around Hotwell Road.

The Property

A property on this Crescent was put up for sale for £375,000. The property was in need of refurbishment throughout. Our research showed that properties on this crescent in good condition sold for up to £500,000 and single-storey flats were selling for up to £200,000.

The Situation

Our research also uncovered that the property was bought by the current owners in 2006 for £343,500. We called the estate agent who explained that a couple with two children had bought the house five years ago with the intention of completing the refurbishment themselves whilst living at the property. The couple had started the refurbishment but had underestimated the time the work would take. After the husband became ill the property had become a burden in terms of both time and money and they decided to sell. Due to the recession and the amount of work required, builders and other investors were offering in the region of £350,000. Selling at this price would have meant that the couple would have lost money. The purchase price was £343,500, Stamp duty at 3% was £10,305, legal costs of buying and selling £3,000-£4,000. This meant the couple would have spent in the region of £360,000 excluding what they had spent on refurbishment.

We calculated the refurbishment costs at between £60,000 and £80,000 depending on whether we were able to get planning permission to convert the basement into a self-contained flat.

Win-Win

We calculated the refurbished value to be £500,000 as a single house, or £550,000 if we could convert the property into a maisonette with a separate basement flat (values of £375,000 & £175,000 respectively). This meant that we could afford to offer the sellers the full asking price and still make a profit of £65,000 - £95,000. We got the planning permission and I am living in the house, the flat is currently being sold and the £175,000+ that it will generate will pay for the £85,000 refurbishment costs and £90,000 deposit for the house/maisonette above.

What have you learned from this case study?

_____

_____

_____

_____

_____

_____

What key actions can you take as a result of your learning?

_____

_____

_____

_____

_____

_____

Chapter 20: Working with the Best – Rachael's Case Study

As my reputation as a great deal maker and options expert grew, I found that more people wanted to work with me. Options had been around for a while and yet securing them seemed to elude the majority; even very successful investors struggled to convince estate agents that they were a good idea. Rachael Wilson, soon to be crowned winner of Mastermind 8 (MM8), had already done two options directly with sellers but was finding agents hard to crack. Rachael knew exactly what she wanted – someone to sit down in front of estate agents with her and explain the benefits of options and why their clients would want to sell this way. She also wanted someone who could answer the agents' questions confidently and without hesitation. Most people approach agents only thinking about themselves, thinking about the portfolio they want to build and the cash-flow that they want to generate. I'll let you into a secret: the agents couldn't care less about you or your portfolio. They care primarily about themselves, then their clients … maybe.

By now I had mastered my strategy and written a short fifteen-minute presentation to lead the agents through. Firstly it focused on the benefits to the agent then, and only then, it moved on to the benefits to the seller. Only at this point are agents willing to listen to what you have to say. I run through all the different reason why sellers, even the savviest and financially astute with higher value properties, would want to sell properties this way.

I taught Rachael the presentation over Skype then gave her a week to practice it before presenting back to me. Rachael is a fast learner so with just a small amount of tweaking we were ready to go. Rachael had been proactive with the agents already and had bought a few properties so they already had respect for her. I made my way to Leeds and we got straight to it after a quick cup of tea. As agreed I presented to the first two agents so that Rachael could observe and chip in with her local knowledge. Then it was crunch time – Rachael's time to present. Bless her, she saved the worst agent for herself; you know they're going to be fun when arms are crossed and their face looks like they are chewing a wasp. Rachael did a great job of leading the presentation and I only chipped in to answer questions as needed. As with all my clients I had taught Rachael not to argue if the agent objects to the concepts raised, and where possible to try to agree with the agent's objections. This may sound odd but how can the agent possibly argue with someone who is agreeing with them? When you use this tactic the agent's resistance seems to melt very quickly. So many people think they need to prove themselves right or win the argument to get the deal. If you look at it from the agent's point of view, would you sell a property to someone who has proved you wrong and beaten you in an argument? I thought not. Anyway, back to the story. By the end of the presentation the agent seemed to have a smile and her arms-folded stance had changed to her frantically copying the summary slide of the type of sellers we were looking for. Was it the great presentation that won it for us or the realisation that we pay the estate agents' fees in the middle of a recession? Probably a bit of both, I guess.

Rachael's Story

I'd been investing in property for just a year so I was still quite new to it although I'd had some fantastic success. I started in October 2010, had no money to invest and I was also unmortgageable, However I managed with help to get 12 properties in just twelve months. I did this using various strategies I'd learned and by working with other people doing Joint Ventures.

I'd already done a few lease options when I decided that I needed to go to the next level and work with Barry. I'd tried to get lease options from estate agents and although I'd got one, they just didn't seem to understand the concept and I wasn't able to convey it effectively. I knew Barry was very successful at getting high yielding lease options and from my experience in NLP and working in sales I knew that for me to be successful I needed to model and copy someone who already was.

Barry was fantastic as he spoke to me several times on Skype and we ran through the presentation he used for agents. He had a go, then I had a go, and this role play really helped me build my confidence. I wasn't expecting him to do this as I thought I would just spend the day with him, so I was really impressed that he took so much time before to make sure I was comfortable and ready for the day.

I arranged the day to see estate agents back to back. These were estate agents that had previously said no to lease options for their vendors but I arranged the appointments with confidence as I knew I was with Barry and knew that they would understand clearly the benefits of lease options.

It was fantastic as all the agents responded really well and this was due to Barry's very easy to understand presentation that helped them clearly to see why they were of benefit. It also helped me to explain the different ways in which lease options can work for people and although I already had experience I learnt some ways which I'd not previously known.

The deals I got were:

Deal 1

Fully licenced and furnished 6 bed HMO
Purchase price £130,000
Monthly lease fee £650
Bills £350
Rental income £1,680
Profit £780
Length 4 years

The owner's son had lived in the property whilst at Uni and then couldn't sell; they had no mortgage and leasing the property to me gave them a better return than they would have got if they put the money in the bank at a poor interest rate.

Deal 2

Purchase price £170,000
Monthly lease fee £900

Rental income £1,800
Profit £900
Length 6 years

2 x 1-bedroom flats and a 3-bedroom duplex.

The owners lived away weren't getting good rent and found it hard to manage, it needed some TLC.

They were happy to do a lease option because they couldn't sell and wanted the hassle gone.

Both sets of owners gave me testimonials to say how they loved lease options!

I would say that my success has been because I'm persistent. I have learnt that I don't know everything, so it's always best to learn from someone else who has already achieved what you are trying to achieve. Thanks Barry, for helping me break through my comfort zone and go for high yielding HMOs.

Rachael Wilson

My Observations and Comments

Wow, what a result! I must admit that after working with Rachael I wondered whether I should be mentoring or just doing deals when those results are possible. I really admire how Rachael was really brave and although she was strapped for cash (as a result of doing eight deals in as many months), she decided to go for the mentoring.

Rachael's investment really paid off as she agreed two deals from the meetings we had during the on-site day of the mentoring program. The cash-flow from the two multi-let properties was £1,680 per month.

Notice how the sellers were both happy; in both cases Rachael was able to give a better return than the sellers would have got if they had sold for full asking price and put the money in the bank. It's a really good idea to get testimonials as Rachael did, as inevitably a seller may be wary of doing something they have not heard of before. If you can show that other people are doing it and are happy with the result, then it will be easier to convince them.

If there was one thing that anyone could learn from Rachael, it is the power of taking massive action. Rachael was already massively successful before I had the pleasure of working with her, and she had achieved this success by taking decisive action, viewing hundreds of properties in total and building great relationships with the agents. Rachael thoroughly deserved to win MM8.

What have you learned from this case study?

_____

_____

_____

_____

_____

What key actions can you take as a result of your learning?

_____

_____

_____

_____

_____

Chapter 21: Around the World and Back – Gillie's Case Study

Gillie won Simon Zutshi's Mastermind programme MM9 exclusively through large option deals during and following on from our mentoring. Here is her story including her first deal.

Gillie's Story

It is true – I have always loved property, my mother said from the age of seven she thought I would be an estate agent.

For me it all started when I was twenty-one years old working for a pittance in a fish farm. I had left school with little to show. For years I'd sat in a classroom bored and then I had travelled to Africa with £30 worth of traveller's cheques. What I experienced during that time moulded part of who I am today, and it was here that a dream in the bush was the start of my property journey. This is a story of its own but resulted in me buying a chalet in the French Alps.

At twenty-one an element of common sense and business acumen set in and by getting a ski company to rent it for five winter seasons, paying me in advance for each of the seasons, the second French Bank I approached (Banque Le Henin) agreed to loan me the money on a fifteen-year repayment mortgage basis.

Part of that same dream in the bush was about disabled children and building up their confidence and self-belief. Having bought the chalet in 1990, I took the first group of disabled children out there in the summer of 1991. SADA was officially registered as a charity in 1994. This has continued to run most years since then.

After five years the ski company's contract ended and I started to manage the bookings for the winter myself and to this day still do. Over the next number of years I designed and had built the house in which I still live with my family. I then looked constantly at other parts of the world and at property that was rustic, romantic and old. I loved old property of many types and eventually bought an old fisherman's cottage in a beautiful part of North Cornwall. Even though good value and in need of renovation, it came at a fair old price and a mortgage that spelt that out. Over the next few years I bought in different countries on developments small and large for the sole purpose of future growth and great returns upon eventual sale. Not long after I went to Canada and bought fourteen acres of beautiful land. Soon I hope to set up the second leg of the charity, building confidence in older children and young adults.

So as you can see, up until that point it was lifestyle and I would be constantly juggling monies to help cover debt on the properties and land that I had bought or built.

As a mother of three young boys, mortgaged up to the hilt and with no liquid capital, I was not about to do anything that would jeopardise what I had worked for or impinge on the life we had built as a family.

I had heard a small amount about 'buy to let investments' and in my 'open minded' sort of way, decided to look into it. It seemed an excellent strategy to create funds in a painless way thus reducing borrowing on other assets and allowing me the opportunity to create a passive income of as much as I wanted, then freeing me to do other things I am passionate about that don't necessarily create an income.

Over the next year I learnt a lot. I learnt there were people to avoid and exceptionally healthy people to be around but most of all I learnt that it wasn't anything to be scared of. Unlike many investment opportunities and plans, it was something I could control … to a point. It was something I could see grow and make choices about. I learnt that the risk factor could be miniscule if crucial rules were followed and I learnt it could be rewarding and fun.

I will be forever grateful that I met people that, as I do, believe that to give is greater than to gain but that in giving we do indeed gain ten-fold. The teachings on Simon Zutshi's Mastermind and accelerator courses and both the Ben and Barry Option course and League of Warriors course, were not just building blocks to help grow investment and to create constant income but were and still are fairly major in the growing of me, my attitudes and my responses.

There is much in life we run from and there is much scepticism surrounding us, but before we say 'it's too good to be true' we need to listen and learn and then and only then weigh up what we consider risk, and see that it is actually … called 'living'.

I did that by investing in myself and am so glad that in ten years I will not be looking back saying 'if only' I had understood it well enough to take that step.

Case Study

I had learnt not to listen to the negative subconscious thoughts and the old belief that motivated sellers didn't exist in Oxford. I had decided I preferred the 'approaching agents' tactic and had built up a rapport with this particular agent. He already knew that I was pursuing a lease option on this large end terrace but had not explained it to the landlord. When I emailed the proposal to the agent I gave two options, 1) a BMV (below market value) purchase offer and 2) a lease option deal. It turns out that the agent didn't actually send the purchase offer over to the landlord. The landlord showed interest in the option and we met without the agent to discuss the structure and on-going process in detail.

The landlord had obviously had the suggested figures and time frame that I had sent over to the agent and he was slightly taken aback that I was happy with profit that to him didn't seem an awful lot. Over the next few days the figures and time frames were thrown back and forth a bit until both the landlord and I were happy with the result.

Now completely happy with the concept and raring to move forward the contract was drawn up.

I proposed to pay £1,800 for a seven-bedroom house with an additional one-bedroom annex bringing in rental of £2,850 or £3,010 Local Housing Allowance (LHA). The house had been on the market at £380,000 and had slowly come down to £350,000 (the landlord had bought it in 2006 for £331,000). I offered to buy it in five years (2015) for £340,000.

We finally agreed on: -
£1,800 a month and £340,000 purchase price at the end of a four-year lease.

The landlord in this case was not especially motivated. However he was tired of the whole buy to let business and was just keen to offload his property. He was delighted to find that the money I was offering him was exactly the profit he had been achieving doing it himself, and would now get the same profit doing nothing himself. This therefore was part of what made the deal a win-win. I was equally as happy as I could see a profit of between £600 and £1,000, depending on the tenant type.

I believe 100% that it was because of the relationship that was built up, the trust and the rapport that sprung out of something that we found in common that created a business relationship that I know will continue.

Gillie's Top Tips

1. Write goals and believe in them.
2. Build Relationships. Learn the correct communication methods and skills that may differ for the different groups of people (i.e., letting agents, estate agents, landlords, home owners, etc)
3. Remember **Will Power** and **Belief** create persistence. Persistence is what instils faith that results in financial success.

Success, I believe, comes from passion and determination, from a totally positive approach and the decision to never stop learning and allowing every tiny success along life's journey to be an experience of its own. These few things have certainly made a difference to the success I have had over the last twenty years.

I do offer coaching and mentoring, if you would like details do please contact me on gillie@sophiainvestments.co.uk

Gillie Barlow

My Observations and Comments

Wow, what a story! I first heard this when Gillie came to speak at the Bristol PIN (property investors network) meeting that I used to run with my business partner

Ben. I love this story and I'll always enjoy hearing or reading it.

Gillie's personal story is so inspiring that it almost makes the option deal that generates £800 a month boring! Gillie had approached us and was keen to acquire properties in her area (an affluent city in the South of England). Gillie was keen to acquire large properties and multi-let them to maximise cash-flow. Gillie was unconvinced that marketing to buy properties below their true market value would be successful. There are motivated sellers in every city that will be willing to sell below market value. There are certainly a lot less motivated sellers in richer areas and this means that marketing to buy properties 20%-40% below market value is not financially viable (the cost of getting a deal is much greater because the conversion rate is so much lower). With this in mind, Gillie was keen to use options to acquire property.

Following our training, Gillie took loads of action and viewed a fair few properties. She generated interest from agents and within a couple of months she had found her first option deal. Was he a desperate seller? No. Was he in a massive rush to sell? No. Did he have little to no equity in the property? No, the mortgage was very small. Was he motivated to get a good deal that worked well for him financially? Most certainly. Gillie's seller is typical of the landlords I deal with, wealthy, very financially astute and wanting to sell to get rid of the hassle rather than being in a desperate need for the money right now.

I'm really impressed with what Gillie has achieved here, Gillie is far too modest to mention the amount of charitable work she does as well as running multiple businesses and a home with 3 children. Most of the time when I speak to Gillie she doesn't seem to know whether she is coming or going, and she still managed to pull off a great deal. Since this deal she has signed options on £2,000,000 worth of property by focusing on big deals. Gillie went on to win Mastermind 9 purely through the option deals she had done during and as a result of our mentoring. With both her and Rachael that was two Mastermind wins in a row for us :-).

What have you learned from this case study?

_____

_____

_____

_____

_____

_____

What key actions can you take as a result of your learning?

_____

_____

_____

_____

_____

_____

Part 2: Developing a Winning Mindset!

Developing a Winning Mindset

Before we get into the details of how you can go out and find yourself some great deals, let's make sure your mind is in the right place. This is even more important than knowing the technical details because without the right mindset you won't have the confidence to sell your idea to the seller or the agent and if you don't believe, then the deals will fall over.

The man who thinks he can

If you think you are beaten, you are;
If you think you dare not, you don't.
If you'd like to win, but think you can't
It's almost a cinch you won't.

If you think you'll lose, you've lost.
For out in the world we find
Success begins with a fellow's will:
It's all in his state of mind.

If you think you're outclassed, you are:
You've got to think high to rise,
You've got to be sure of yourself before
You'll ever win that prize.

Life's battles don't always go
To the stronger or faster man,
But sooner or later the man who wins
Is the one who thinks he can.

Walter D Wintle

Chapter 22: Belief

Belief is the cornerstone to all success. Belief comes first and success comes second. If you wait for success before you believe in yourself you will be waiting a long time. So many people who live in affluent cities don't believe they can get deals; by deals I mean discounted property sold below the market value or lease options where the price is fixed now but the property is bought in the future. These people then buy properties elsewhere in the country with great yields, etc., etc. The vast majority of people I have met who have done this have not made anything like the returns they expected. Those were the more fortunate ones; many of the others got ripped off by sharks, through paying money for deals that never existed. If you believe that you can get great deals in your area it will happen, but you have to believe it first. I'm certainly not saying it will be easy but it will be worth the effort. The capital appreciation of properties in the affluent areas will be greater and will happen sooner than in poorer areas. London will be the first to grow as we come out of this recession followed by the Home Counties and other major cities. Areas in the North have suffered greatly and because a lot of the manufacturing employment will never return, the

North (except for the major cities) will recover very slowly.

It is easy to believe in yourself when everyone is behind you. You must believe in yourself even when everyone else thinks you're stark raving mad! I once decided to run a half marathon. I already did weight training and circuit training regularly and didn't want to give these up. The challenge was that whilst doing these I wouldn't have any time for running training. I decided that I didn't need to go running as I was already fit and healthy. Everyone I told said that I was mad. They doubted I could run that long without stopping. They thought I was bonkers when I told them I planned to complete it between one hour forty-five minutes and one hour fifty minutes. This was about twenty minutes faster than most of my friends who had done a half marathon or two that they had trained for. It's not like everyone was particularly negative about it, these were good friends who were supportive and genuinely concerned. Admittedly this was to be the first time I had been for a run for over a year but I BELIEVED that I would do it. The more people who told me that I couldn't, the more I was determined to complete it – and within the time I had told them. I was so convinced I would do it that when I told people and they laughed at the fact that I was doing it without specific training, I truly thought that these people were crazy, even a little 'special', as this was simply a done deal on my part! They were laughing hysterically at what to me was just a fact. Part of me loves to hear people say that you can't do something, it makes me want to prove them wrong even more and the victory is all the more sweet.

I took a stopwatch to the race as I wanted to keep track of my time and make sure I was on course. I didn't have any of the posh/designer running clothes that other runners had and I didn't have any pockets to put the stopwatch in so I tied it to the draw string on my shorts. I set off with my friend Claire who had warned me against not training for it. One mile into the race I realised that my three-four year old trainers rubbed – that blister was going to grow a bit in the next twelve miles! After about four miles I began to get a bit bored and decided to pick up the pace a bit assuming my friend would keep up. I looked round a minute later and she was gone. I went to take a look at my stopwatch; it had stopped after thirty minutes. I now had no idea how I was doing against my target. I kept a pace that was hard but sustainable, a metaphor for business actually. The event was a lot more enjoyable than when I'd been running previously; people lined the streets and there was a real sense of occasion. This really spurred me on, the atmosphere was great. I picked up the pace further for the last two miles. As I came round a corner I saw the finish line, and being a man I had to go for a sprint finish! I looked up at the clock: one hour forty-seven minutes – smack bang in the middle of the time range I had targeted. This was no coincidence, I had visualised this whenever someone doubted I could do it! I learnt two lessons that day:

1. You can do anything if you set your mind to it and believe in yourself.
2. You should put Vaseline on anything that might rub/chafe

The other time when I needed great belief was when things were really tight financially. Everyone told me to get a job, even my coach suggested getting a job, and my mentor as well. I knew we could make it without resorting to that and I would really have felt like I was a failure if I'd gone back to work. It was great to have my best friend as my business partner during these tough times. Nobody takes more action than Ben when the pressure is on, he is relentless! We work really well together, we're like-minded guys and at the same time we have very different strengths and weaknesses. Ben is a people person; he hates numbers, strategy and most of all details. The man is a genius with people though; I've never seen anyone have more success with people than Ben. He really knows what to say to make them tick.

Chapter 23: Demand More

"Most of you don't want success as much as you want to sleep."

Eric Thomas

At the time of writing I have just completed my first full marathon. I trained a bit for this one, running on average once per week for the few months running up to the event, simply running a little bit further each time I went out then easing off as I came up to the big day. People say that they don't have time for exercise. Successful people simply demand more from themselves.

Many high achievers in business run marathons, triathlons and so on in their spare time. These are some of the busiest people you'll ever meet and yet they still find time to exercise. These people demand more from themselves. Whilst training for the marathon, I'm writing this book, running a multi-million pound portfolio, running training seminars, mentoring individuals, completing an option deal nearly every month and spending most weekends with my girlfriend who lives two hours away. I'm also working on my first million pound deal. I'm not writing this to show off (ok, well just a little bit). I'm challenging you to demand more from yourself. We all have twenty-four hours in a day and yet some people achieve so much more than others. Richard Branson has the same twenty-four hours that you or I have and look what he achieves in a day.

Chapter 24: Persistence

"Never give in, never, never, never, never, in nothing great or small, large or petty, never give in except to convictions of honour and good sense. Never yield to force; never yield to the apparently overwhelming might of the enemy."

Winston Churchill

You don't fail until you give up. It's that simple! You may make a lot of mistakes, you will learn from every one of them. Admittedly you might need to make the same mistake a few times but then the hardest learnt and most expensive lessons are the best. If you want to read a great story about persistence I suggest reading James Dyson's book "Against All Odds". Despite having great inventions James really struggled to get them off the ground.

Chapter 25: Love What You Do

"Without passion you don't have energy, without energy you have nothing."

Donald Trump

Until you go into business for yourself you have no idea how little you actually know. Business can be tough, especially in a recession. Unless you love and are passionate about what you are doing you won't last the course. I can tell you from experience that it is a real roller coaster ride; there are massive highs and even deeper lows. I also believe that having your own business is the best way to live your life, you experience so much more than you do in the corporate 9.00am to 5.00pm. Just make sure you're passionate about the business to ensure you will be the most successful.

Chapter 26: Focus on What You Want – Focus on the Solution

You achieve what you focus on so it makes sense to focus on what you really want. If you focus on the problems that you are experiencing then you will get stuck in them and you will even attract more problems. It is key to always focus on the solution. This seems obvious. In theory it is simple; in practice however when you have a big problem it's hard not to worry about it. This is when you need to show resolve and keep the end goal in mind.

Chapter 27: Study Success

If you want to be a mathematician you study mathematics. If you want to be successful you must study success and successful people. Whether you choose practical self-help books or prefer to read autobiographies of successful people I believe that there is something out there for everyone. So many people tell me that they don't have time to read yet these are the very same people who spend a couple of hours a day in front of the TV. Someone once suggested to me that you should put a picture of all of your goals in front of the TV, then you have to physically put your goals aside to watch it. Let's face it, this is what you do every time you watch TV anyway. I'm not saying that you should never take some time out but you certainly shouldn't do it every day just by default regardless of what's actually on the TV at the time. Pick up a book instead! I know of not one person who has expressed on their death bed that they wished they had watched more TV!

Another great way to study success is through audio programmes. Most people commute at least some distance every day. Why listen to Chris Moyles moaning when you could be listening to books by

Richard Branson, Donald Trump or even Winston Churchill.

One of the greatest gifts that I get from books is a look into the writer's mind. It's often not the facts that I learn that are the most valuable, but to see how that super successful person thinks. Great books also have an amazing impact on your state of mind. If you're having a hard time and you read about how Trump came back from having $900,000,000 of debt to being a multi-billionaire, suddenly your troubles no longer seem insurmountable. The inspiration in these books is more valuable than any information, and a good book will be much more thrilling than any TV programme. Who affects your mindset on a daily basis? The likes of Donald Trump or Eastenders' Pat Butcher.

My top ten books
Losing My Virginity: Richard Branson
The Art of the Deal: Donald Trump
Think Big & Kick Ass: Donald Trump
The Success Principles: Jack Canfield
7 Habits of Highly Effective People: Stephen Covey
Winning: Clive Woodward
Tackling Life: Jonny Wilkinson
How to be Rich J. Paul Getty
Rich Dad Poor Dad: Robert Kiyosaki
The Real Deal: James Caan

Chapter 28: Play to your Strengths

Very few people are good at everything. Let's face it, doing what you are not good at is miserable. It will take you three times as long and you still won't do as good a job as someone who is naturally talented in that area. When you start out in business you will most likely need to do a lot of the work yourself but the sooner you can focus on your strengths, the sooner your success will grow.

If you are unsure of your strengths it is a good idea to ask your friends, family and other people who are close to you. There are also lots of profiling tests that can help you understand this. Wealth Dynamics is a great profiling tool to help you to understand your strengths from a business point of view. This test will help you discover what you should do to be successful in business. For example, my profiles are Trader, Accumulator and Deal Maker so it is easy to see why I have been successful building my wealth through property.

Chapter 29: Who do you Associate with?

"You are, or will become, the average of the five people you associate with the most."

Brian Carruthers

I first heard this theory a few years ago and I must admit it didn't sit at all well with me. A property and motivational speaker told me about it. I felt a little like I was being asked to ditch my friends if they weren't heading in the same direction that I was. I didn't act on the suggestions that I should change my associations at the time as it seemed very shallow. Looking back I see that I naturally started to spend more time with people who were looking to build wealth, success and happiness. The conversations were more invigorating and inspiring and the energy levels were lots higher. Now I actively look to spend time with like-minded people. Recently my business partner and I went snowboarding for a week with Simon Zutshi and a few other millionaires. The conversations on the ski lifts, in the hot tub and around the open fire were amazing. It's fascinating how much these people can get done. They play at a level that is much higher than most. One of the guys is working on a social enterprise that aims to eradicate poverty. You certainly don't get those conversations in the local pub!

A Final Word on Mindset: Let Go of the Past

Many people fail to achieve the success that they want and deserve because their past is holding them back and stopping them from achieving their full potential. It's a great shame not only for these people but also for those around them who won't experience their true greatness. For all concerned it is essential to get this out of the way once and for all. If you feel there is something holding you back and you would like to deal with this I would recommend a great resource: theleagueofwarriors.com where you can download a free video series to get you started.

Part 3: Securing Lease Options and Running Your Property Business

Chapter 30: An Introduction to Lease Options

What is a Lease Option?

A lease option contract is a lease agreement where the leaseholder leases the property and has the exclusive option but not the obligation to purchase the property during the lease period. The owner is however obliged to sell the property if the option holder decides to buy

How can you benefit from leases and lease options?

There are two ways you benefit from lease option contracts. The first way is to rent the property out for more than you pay on the monthly lease fee and therefore you make positive monthly cash-flow; this should be a minimum of £500 per month and is often up to £1,000 a month. The other way you can make money is through the capital growth of the property over and above what you have agreed to pay. Generally when we sign a lease option contract, we agree to buy the property for the value that it is worth at that time. This means that if we increase the value of the property or the market increases we will benefit from that growth.

What if you are not in a position to buy at the end of the lease?

Lease option contracts are assignable, which means you can benefit from them even if you don't buy the property yourself. You can do this by instructing the sale of the property and selling it for more than you have agreed to buy it from the seller. The contract states that you will benefit from the difference in what you have agreed to pay and the price that you sell for.

For example, if you agree to pay today's market value of £200,000 for a property in six years' time, the value in six years' time may be 25% higher than it is today. So in six years' time, the property would be worth £250,000. If for whatever reason you decide not to buy the property you could sell it on the open market for the full market value of £250,000 and make a £50,000 profit. Of course you would have to pay legal costs and maybe an estate agent but you would still be left with near £45,000.

How is a lease option constructed? What are the variables?

Term / Duration − How long should the lease be?

The term of the option must be acceptable to both you and the seller. The term you require is dependent on your objective for the particular property.

If you are negotiating a lease option in order to benefit from the capital growth of the property, then the option should be a minimum of five years but ideally longer as the market is uncertain.

If you are using a lease option to control and access the property to increase its value through refurbishment or planning permission, then the length of the lease would not need to be so long. For example if you are just looking to complete a light refurbishment this may take as little as three months for the refurbishment and a further three months to complete the purchase or sale.

It is advisable to make the lease option six to twelve months longer than you think is required so that you are protected against delays.

Upfront option fee – Should I pay an upfront fee?

Sellers may require an upfront fee from you to cover their costs or to give them security that you are serious. I believe that it is fair to cover a seller's costs initially, because they won't receive money from the sale at this stage. You may agree to pay these costs as part of the deal or agree to pay them upfront and have them taken off of the sale price. I would avoid paying additional fees to the seller to give security; instead this security/reassurance should be provided through building a relationship and doing what you say you will do.

Monthly option fee – Should I pay a monthly fee and if so what should I pay?

Many investors agree only to cover the costs of the seller's mortgage. I feel that this can restrict the properties you can buy using options as only really desperate/ motivated sellers would agree to this. I feel the best way to calculate what you can offer is to work out your costs and how much profit you want to make each month. Subtract this figure from the rent you will be able to achieve and you will have your maximum monthly lease fee, this is the figure that you can't go above, not what you issue.

The purchase price – How much should I pay?

Many investors will only pay what is outstanding on the mortgage. Although this philosophy will give you the best profit, it may limit the amount and quality of property that you can buy. If sellers are agreeing to a delayed sale they may expect to get today's market value for the property. If you are prepared to pay more than what is owed on the mortgage, this will give you a better position to negotiate from.

Generally the price (your offer) should be in the range between the outstanding mortgage and today's market value. I generally calculate my maximum offer by calculating my costs and required profit/equity gain and subtract these from what I predict the property will be worth at the time of purchase. It's advisable to take a pessimistic view of capital growth when making these calculations.

Here is an example to help you:

Value at time of purchase (£200,000) - Costs (£20,000) and Profit (£15,000) = Offer price (£165,000)

There is a market for buying properties that are currently in negative equity. If you agree to buy a property for more than it's currently worth, I feel the other features of the deal should be favourable. By this I mean the cash-flow should be good – ideally at least £250 for a single let or £500 from a multi-let, and the term of the option should be longer to give more time for market growth. For every 5% of negative equity you should add two years to the option duration.

In certain circumstances it may be acceptable to give the seller a percentage of the market growth if they require this to agree to the deal. If you agree to do this I would advise limiting this to 5% to 15% of the value increase.

Value at time of purchase (£200,000)
Original purchase price (£150,000)
Equity growth = (£50,000)
Vendor's share @ 5% of equity growth = (£2,500)
Purchase price including seller's share of growth = £152,500

Always fix the price rather than agreeing to buy at a discount of the value at the time of sale. Agreeing to a discount would mean you will be paying more for the property if you improve it in any way.

Negotiating terms – a quick tip

Sellers will often want to negotiate when making an offer. It's advisable to add a year to the required term and offer 10% less than your required monthly fee and purchase price to allow for negotiation.

Don't give concessions - trade them!

If a seller insists on more money, for example, you should insist on a longer term and or a smaller monthly fee. If you just agree, the seller is likely to then start negotiating on the other terms and the deal quickly become unprofitable.

When are options not the best solution?

Options are not the best solution if the seller needs a significant amount of money now. If the seller is selling because they need a large sum of money it's advisable that they sell through a more traditional route.

This is all relative of course; putting £10,000 down on day one is not advisable if the property is only worth £100,000 and the yearly cash-flow is £3,000. However if the property is a £250,000 multi-let that generates £15,000 a year cash-flow then you may consider paying a £10,000 option fee to the seller if this is the only way the option can work for him or her.

As a general rule the total acquisition and renovation costs should be recouped through the first year's cash-flow.

Costs – can you really buy a house for a pound?

There are people selling lease options courses using headlines like 'Buy a house for a pound'. Is this really possible? Can you really buy a house for a pound? Not exactly, you can buy the option for a pound but not the house. You have to buy the option because a transaction needs to take place. Because investors always like to keep costs to a minimum they will generally pay the nominal fee of a pound.

What's the reality? What can you expect to pay out?

The reality is that as well as the much talked about £1 option fee, you will also need to pay for a solicitor to draw up a contract on your behalf as an absolute bare minimum. Solicitors cost anything between £300 and £3,000 depending upon who the solicitor is and how complex the option agreement is – another reason to keep it simple.

Do I really need to get a solicitor? Can't I just get the contracts off the internet?

I wholeheartedly recommend using a solicitor to ensure that the contracts are legally correct. Every situation and every contract is different, therefore getting a contract off the internet is a risky idea. There is a lot at stake; there will often be between £20,000 and £200,000 equity in the property by the end of the option term and so it's not worth scrimping on the initial cost which is usually below £800.

Does the seller really need their own solicitor too?

It's essential that the seller has a solicitor to protect their interests. Your contracts should be fair and mutually beneficial and it's important that the seller knows exactly what they are signing and is completely happy. The other really important reason that the seller needs their own solicitor is that at the end of the contract they may forget that the lease option agreement was mutually beneficial, and they might feel it's unfair that you want to buy their house for significantly less than it's worth at the time of purchase. For example you may agree to buy someone's house for the £210,000 that's outstanding on the mortgage, rather than the £200,000 that it's worth when they signed the contract because the house is in negative equity. If at the end of the lease agreement the house is worth £250,000, they may easily forget the favour that you did them by ridding them of the burden of this house and they may try to contest the option agreement in court. If this happens and they didn't have legal advice when signing the contract the judge might well rule the contract invalid. In this situation if there has been no legal representation for the seller at the point that the contract was signed, they could easily make out that they were in a vulnerable position and that you pressured them to sign the contract.

Should I pay for the seller's solicitor?

Many investors offer to pay for the seller's solicitors as a goodwill gesture and also because most investors are signing contracts with sellers who are in financial difficulty. I much prefer that the seller pays for their own legal representation for three reasons:

1. So that the seller is committed to the agreement. It's very frustrating if you have paid the seller's legal fees and they then back out of the deal leaving you out of pocket. If the seller is financially committed they are less likely to pull out.
2. If the seller has paid for their own legal representation then it will be more difficult for them to dispute the contract later when their house is worth more than you are paying for it.
3. So that I don't have to pay the expense myself.

I've heard that I need to use a solicitor that specialises in this type of contract, is this true?

There are a few solicitors in the UK that specialise in option contracts on residential property and it's a really good idea to use one of these. This is because the solicitors that specialise in this type of transaction have templates that they use and adjust to the individual merits of your case. This means that they can write the contracts quickly and they will often do it for a fixed fee. Since solicitors charge in the region of £200 an hour, getting a solicitor to write a contract from the start could be very expensive. Also if the solicitor doesn't have the necessary experience they may miss certain clauses.

I've heard that for options to work I must insist that the seller uses the solicitor that I tell them to use?

It is advisable but not essential that the seller uses a solicitor from your panel of recommended solicitors. Solicitors with experience will act more quickly and will be more thorough. Solicitors that don't understand option agreements may suggest that they are not legal or they may advise the seller against the transaction. This is more likely to happen if they believe that their client is in a vulnerable position. I have signed an option agreement with a solicitor who wanted to dispose of a property and was happy to act for himself. I have also agreed option contracts with sellers who insist on using their family solicitors and have not yet had a deal fall through. This is because I ensure that the agreements are truly win-win and because I often deal with wealthy landlords who are not considered vulnerable. In most cases the sellers are as keen to do the deals as I am.

Why should I invest in multi-let properties? Aren't they more work than properties rented out to families?

Multi-lets are more work than single lets but they produce a lot more profit. We have a number of single lets and have found that one single let house produces roughly the same profit as one room in a multi let. This is usually £100-£200 per month. For example, a multi-let with five rooms will produce £500-£1,000 profit, whereas a house let to a family will make £100-£200. When most people decide to invest in property they don't realise that they will need twenty to thirty single let properties to produce reasonable income. In comparison four to six high cash-flowing multi-let properties will produce a similar income.

Aren't multi-lets expensive?

Generally houses suitable for renting room by room are more expensive than traditional buy to let houses for two reasons:

1. The houses are larger than traditional houses; they generally need five or more large lettable rooms as well as communal space, a reasonable size kitchen and at least two bathrooms.
2. Both young professionals and students like to be situated in up and coming areas containing

pubs, bars and coffee shops, not to mention good transport links, etc.

Both the criteria above come at a premium so you can expect to pay a bit more for the properties. But think about it, where would you prefer to own properties? Which properties will experience the most growth, the ones in the back end of nowhere or the ones in up and coming areas?

Who to do option deals with?

With options being such a win-win solution for both buyers and sellers I really don't understand why, when investors consider acquiring properties this way, they tend towards the same type of properties as they would be buying below market value. There is often a reason people are willing to sell Below Market Value (BMV); the properties are hard to sell because they are in areas where people wouldn't ideally like to buy. If you can create true win-win deals with sellers why would you restrict yourself in this way? Why not go for big houses in the best areas in town? Providing you can make the deal stack up, there is nothing stopping you. Why do deals on six new-build/negative equity flats when you could get the same profit from one multi-let in a great part of town that will be popular with young professionals and will be subject to much greater capital appreciation?

Another reason to be wary of doing deals with similar properties as you would target for Below Market Value purchases is that you will be dealing with similar owners. Maybe it's wrong to stereotype, however a lot of people in these situations are not the best at managing money. It's not necessarily their fault as they have probably not had the best role models and have never been taught basic money management skills. Nevertheless, I wouldn't be rushing to jump into bed with one of these people (financially jumping in to bed of course). Let's imagine you're at a property networking event, and someone approaches you and asks you to participate in a joint venture (JV) on a deal they have, sounds good so far, right? Then they tell you they have had the property for a few years and have got into trouble with it, they explain that they are in arrears and have been threatened with repossession. As a result their credit rating is shot. How keen are you to do a joint venture with them now? I've always thought of options as a JV and as a result I've never felt it would be a good idea to enter into such a venture with someone on the verge of bankruptcy.

Who would be your ideal JV partner? A solicitor? A fellow property investor? An accountant? A consultant?

What if it were possible to acquire properties using options from these people? The good news is that this is possible and we have done deals with all of the above.

What are the benefits of dealing with wealthy landlords?

You can talk on the level to these people as they have a good understanding of finance and are generally better educated. You can quickly come to a win-win agreement that you are sure is mutually beneficial. These people generally don't opt to use the solicitor that you suggest, instead they tend to use a family solicitor that they have used before and are comfortable with. Many people will only agree a lease option if the seller agrees to use the suggested solicitor. This puts off all but the most desperate sellers. We are happy for the seller to use their own solicitors because we want them to be completely happy. We have found that if the deal is truly win-win the solicitor will have no reason to object. We are yet to have a deal fall over because of the seller's solicitor, even though only one seller has used one of the well-known specialist option solicitors we'd recommend. The other less obvious benefit of this is that the seller is much less likely to try to find a way out of the option at time of exercising the option and if they do they are highly unlikely to succeed.

Chapter 31: Sourcing Properties

Getting the Best out of Estate Agents

I used to hate estate agents; they always seemed to make things hard work. They would never want to ask the sellers about the information that I thought I needed and they weren't very keen to put forward my offers. Admittedly these were very low offers because when I started investing I was doing what everyone else in the property investment scene was doing – offering 70% of what the property was worth. If I couldn't do this I would try to get them to agree to an option deal if they were in negative equity and had no other choice.

Looking back, I now understand where they were coming from; they didn't want to ask the sellers personal questions such as:

Were they in arrears with their mortgage?
Were they in danger of being repossessed?
How much did they owe on their mortgage?
How much was their monthly mortgage payment?
I can also understand why they weren't so keen to put forward an offer equal to 70% of what the house was

worth. These were people's homes we were dealing with and unless they put the offers across very tactfully they could be extremely insulting. Additionally, of course, their commission would be lower!

If there was one group of people that I used to find more frustrating than the agents, it was the guy who seemed to be getting all the good deals. These people also seemed to be friends with the agents. It just didn't seem fair, I didn't feel that we were playing on a level playing field; they were picking up the bargains before I even got to see them, before they even got onto the market. My frustration existed for a while with us only picking up the odd deal once in a blue moon. The more we familiarised ourselves with the agents, the more frequently we started to pick up deals, then one day I looked up and realised that I had become one of 'those guys'. So how did it happen? The key factor was that I persisted. Since the property market crash there had been loads of people trying to cash in by picking up bargains, but most people just don't have the staying power. This is probably why estate agents don't take 'newbies' too seriously. Also, why would an agent give a property to someone who has never done a deal with them before, instead of the guy who buys regularly and has a great track record? If the agent is dealing with a motivated seller they will want to be sure that they won't get let down. How else can you get the agent on side?

Do What You Say You Will Do

This is so simple and so easy to do yet it is also easy not to do. If you want credibility with the agent you need to stick to your word. If you say you'll put an offer forward in the morning then make sure you do. Everything you do sends out signals and you need to make sure you're sending the correct signals. If you don't follow through on your promise the agent may consciously or subconsciously decide that your word is not good; if you have done this then you are likely to mess them around later down the line too. If you delay too long you'll also make them look bad in front of the seller who is keen to get feedback. If you are busy and won't be in a position to offer until after the weekend then just tell them. It's better to under promise and over deliver. Things do crop up and there will be times that you aren't able to do your research and so on, and can't put your offer forward. If this is the case you will need to communicate this to them to keep them up to date.

Let them be the Boss

If you think of an ultra-successful property developer you would probably think of Donald Trump. What this guy has achieved is incredible; he's a real big shot and a great inspiration. Generally it's a good idea to copy what your mentors do but if you think going into the agent and playing the big shot will work you're in for a surprise. First you need to earn the respect that Donald Trump has. Being arrogant won't win you any friends and certainly won't make estate agents warm to you. It's a great idea to remember that you're on their territory and to act accordingly. Estate agents often want to be in charge and I suggest you let them; property investment is not about winning the competition for the biggest ego, it's about getting rich and more importantly it about becoming the person that can achieve the lofty goals you set. Let the agent be the guy who's in charge and you can be the guy that gets quietly rich.

Wealth is not a Swear Word

On the subject of wealth, I would like to share my views. Many people think it's wrong to be rich. I believe that money is neither good nor bad; it is simply a measure of commercial value. Money can be used for many great things; the more you make the more good you can do.

Presenting to Estate Agents

To have the best chance with estate agents it's important that you take time to explain exactly what you want and more importantly what's in it for them, and the sellers, and why they should work with you. The order in which you present this is vitally important. You could eloquently explain exactly why sellers would want to sell this way but unless the agent has bought in they will barely be listening. The first thing you need to explain is what the benefits to the estate agent are. Then and only then can you move on to the benefits to the seller and only after that should you explain why they should work with you. The estate agent doesn't really care about you, and in truth many won't really care about the seller until they know that their own needs are being met.

Educating and Re-educating Estate Agents

Even if you go to estate agents and explain that you want large properties with at least five lettable rooms there will be some agents that phone you the very next day trying to sell you a studio flat! Although this can be frustrating it is important not to rule the property out but instead it's a great idea to reaffirm exactly what you are looking for. Don't give up, just persist and keep telling them until they get it.

Reward Good Behaviour

As soon as you get the deal through an agent it's really important to reward all of their hard work. Although generally we agree to pay their fees I still think it's important to reward them. The majority of the agency fee goes to the company and the agent will get a relatively small commission. I'm not talking about a brown envelope stuffed with money reward – for most reputable agents this would only ruin your reputation. I'm talking about half a dozen bottles of wine. Many agents will share this with their colleagues and all of a sudden you'll have six agents looking out for deals for you!

Chapter 32: Managing your Property Portfolio

The Importance of Finding Good Tenants!

Property management isn't the sexy side of the business. Let's face it, the best part of property investment is creating the deal and landing yourself a massive property in a great part of town, the kind of property that makes people think *"how the hell did he pull that off?"*. In property investment the deal doesn't make you money. The bit that makes you the money is managing well to ensure you get a great return on your investment. Managing well ensures tenants stay for longer, they pay their rent in full and on time and they respect you and the property.

Marketing for Tenants

Your marketing method will depend on your target market. Since our tenants range between the ages eighteen and thirty and are either students or working professionals, they generally look for rooms on the internet.

Gumtree

Gumtree will allow you to advertise one or two rooms for free but if you want to advertise many more you will need to pay them a fee as they now charge agents to use the site. The fee at time of printing is £50. We have had limited success using Gumtree. The prospective tenants aren't always of the best quality and often take ages to respond to emails and texts. Additionally, they often don't have the required rent and deposit to move in.

EasyRoomMate

www.easyroommate.com is a site dedicated to helping tenants find rooms, and landlords find tenants. Since this is a dedicated and paid for service the tenants are usually more serious about moving and tend to be of better quality than those found on Gumtree.

SpareRoom

www.spareroom.co.uk, like easyroommate, is a site dedicated to helping tenants find rooms, and landlords find tenants. Again, since this is a dedicated and paid for service the tenants are usually more serious about moving and tend also to be of better quality than those found on Gumtree.

Viewings

Viewings are the most important part in getting a feel for prospective tenants. Although viewings are intended for tenants to view the property it gives you a chance to meet and interact with the potential tenant and allows you to see if they would fit into the group dynamic of the household.

This is a great time to get some basic information and background history, which may indicate whether or not the individual would make a reliable, trustworthy tenant.

Useful questions:
Why are they looking to move?
When are they are looking to move in?
Where have they moved from?
Are they new to the area?

It is crucial to be personable and friendly on a viewing as it helps the potential tenant feel at ease.

Be sure to highlight all the positive features of the property, whether that is the en suite bathroom, the easy going housemates or the great transport links and location. Finally, make sure you ask the potential tenant if they have any questions, as sometimes information given while touring the property will be forgotten.

Referencing

Referencing tenants is very easy to do; the problem is that it's also easy not to do. It's crazy not to speak to their current landlord and their employer to check the tenant out. The challenge is that a landlord wanting to get rid of a bad tenant may give them a glowing reference, which is why it's a great idea to go to the previous landlord to get an honest opinion.

Credit Checking

Credit checking is so easy and straightforward it would be silly not to do it. You simply need to obtain National Insurance number, date of birth, previous address and signed consent to carry out the checks from the prospective tenant. You can then do the credit check online in two minutes on the National Landlords Association (NLA) website www.landlords.org.uk. This costs £8 for members or £12 for non-members so is a no brainer.

Credit checking and referencing may prove inconclusive. Some tenants will say they are coming from their parents' and people will often have blotches on their credit record. Many professional people with great references and a good credit worthy check will be looking for their own place because they have a good job. I would advise to be cautious when taking on tenants you are not sure about. A bad tenant can take six months to get rid of and could cost six months' rent plus court costs, as it takes this long to evict them. So the total cost could be £370 x 6 + £175 court cost + £120 bailiff fee = £2,515. This cost assumes that you do all the legal paperwork yourself and represent yourself in court. If you wish to use a solicitor this is likely to cost another £1,000. This is why we would always prefer to have an empty room than a bad tenant.

Maintenance

Ideally you want to have little to do with this apart from ensuring that the houses are kept in good order and the bills aren't too high. We have a great relationship with our maintenance guy; he is also our longest serving tenant. We have got to the stage where we trust him and are happy for him to deal directly with the tenants. It's now his phone number that is on the notice boards rather than ours. Most of our tenants don't have my phone number now, which allows me great freedom to lead the business rather than have it lead me.

Trusting your Gut!

Firstly I would never discriminate against anyone because of their sex, race, religion or sexuality. It is however very important to find someone who will get on with the other housemates. We once had a complaint about a male tenant changing his tights in the kitchen. Confronting him about it was an interesting conversation. It is crucial to trust your gut when doing viewings. In the past, when in a rush to fill houses, we took tenants that we were not completely sure of. About 50% of the time they turned out to be fine. The other 50% are the problem. Possibly a big problem! The cost of a bad tenant can be massive and we would rather have no tenant than a bad one.

Fees

Letting property will cost you in terms of both time and money. Even if you do all the work yourself there is still the cost of credit checking (£8-£12) and the cost of protecting the deposit with the deposit protection scheme (£30), so as a bare minimum you should aim to pass these costs on to the tenant. Ideally you should also charge a fee to cover the costs of viewing and administration. It worth checking what other landlords are doing in the area to find out what tenants would expect to pay. Be careful not to charge an amount that will put off tenants as this will cost you more in the long run in terms of time for additional viewings and money through missed rent. We charge tenants a fee of £50, £38 of this is spent on credit checking and deposit protection and £12 goes towards the cost of the employee who organises the contracts and the referencing.

Communal Space

Do tenants really need it or can I turn all rooms into bedrooms to maximise rent?

In my opinion if you want to create a happy house where you can maximise the profit you should always have communal space. It's easy to be seduced by the idea of an extra £300-£500 rent from the extra bedroom you could create but in reality the lack of communal space will reduce the rent on each of the rooms. Living in just one room is also a depressing way to live and unhappy tenants tend to move on as soon as the fixed term of the tenancy expires. This means that you will have the extra expenses for the void period (when the room is empty between tenants) and also the time that it takes you to re-market, conduct viewings and do the administration of the new tenancy.

Who Covers the Bills?

Young professionals renting a room and living with strangers don't want the hassle of sorting out the bills. It is much more attractive for the tenant and simple for you as the landlord if you cover the bills yourself and include this cost within the room rental figure.

Student sharers who come as a group but pay individually will be happy to cover their own bills. When moving groups of tenants in, it is essential that you inform the utility companies that they have moved in and give them the tenants' details to ensure you don't find yourself paying the bills. Some councils insist that the landlord of a HMO is responsible for council tax. Since full time students are exempt you must get them all to provide details of their courses and send this information to the council using an exemption form.

Top Ten Things to be Wary of ...

1. People who want to move in immediately.
2. Prospective tenants whose parents, ex-girlfriends/boyfriends or ex-landlords are helping to move in or offload.
3. Anyone who acts irritably or looks shifty.
4. People whose story changes or doesn't stack up.
5. People who are not punctual.
6. Anyone who struggles to produce the rent, deposit and any fees.
7. Prospective tenants who complain a lot.

8. Shy people who don't engage in conversation – they may not make good housemates for the other tenants.
9. Anyone unable to produce references.
10. Definitely people who fail credit checks.

Chapter 33: Top 12 Legal Questions – Expertly Answered by my Options Solicitor

Are Options Legal?

Options have been around for a very long time. They are recognised in England and Wales as enforceable contracts for the sale of land. The buyer still needs to ensure that each clause in an option does not fall foul of any laws, e.g. unfair contract terms, and does not pressure the seller to sign. The simplest way around the last point is to supply the documents seven to fourteen days before the proposed date for signing and ensure he has legal advice.

What if the Seller Dies?

The seller's estate will be bound by the contract, so his personal representatives will have to honour the terms of the contract and sell the property to you should you choose to exercise the contract.

What if the Seller Goes Bankrupt?

If the seller is bankrupt when he enters into the contract, the contract will be void and unenforceable.

If the seller is made bankrupt after the date of the contract, his interest in the property will vest in the official receiver or the seller's trustee in bankruptcy (TIB). The TIB has powers to apply to the court to end the option. If this happens, you would be left with no option. You would have a claim against the seller for breach of contract but it is rarely worthwhile suing a bankrupt to recover financial losses.

If the TIB does nothing, you will be able to exercise the option as normal but should serve the option notice on the TIB.

What if the Seller Changes their Mind?

The seller cannot change his mind once he has granted the option. However, he may refuse to comply with the contract terms. If this happens, you have to decide whether to risk spending a lot of money taking the seller to court to obtain an order for specific performance of the contract.

You should ensure that the seller receives legal advice before signing the option, so that he can't later say he didn't understand what he was signing.

Are there circumstances under which a judge would overturn the option agreement and side with the seller? A court may refuse to order a seller to perform the contract. This would probably only happen if the court believed the seller was under undue influence to sign or was not of sound mind at the time of signing. The seller would need to provide evidence to support such arguments. Most contracts should be enforceable.

What if the Seller Disappears?

If a seller disappears, you have an issue obtaining title on completion, as the seller won't be around to sign the transfer deed. You should obtain a power of attorney at the outset, so that you (or someone else) can sign on behalf of the seller. Joint seller must appoint more than one attorney, so if there are two sellers, you will need two attorneys.

What if I Miss a Payment?

This will depend on the terms of the contract. A well drafted agreement will allow some time to pay before the seller can terminate the agreement.

What can be Included in the Option Agreement?

You can include any terms that are legal. If you want

authority to do something to the property or to obtain planning permission you should include such authority in the contract. If you want the seller to do something such as pay the mortgage or the insurance premium, you should include an obligation to do so. Alternatively, you may wish to prevent the seller from borrowing more from the lender or selling to a third party. If there is a later a breach of these terms by the seller, you may be able to bring a claim to recover your loss suffered as a result.

How much Legal Information do I Need to Know before Doing an Option?

It is usually best to stick to doing what you do best and leave the legal work to your solicitor.

Do I Need to Use a Solicitor to Write an Option Agreement?

Technically you don't need a solicitor. However, if you want to be sure the agreement is properly drafted and registered against the seller's title, you should use a solicitor. For a relatively small fee, you will have the protection of the solicitor's professional indemnity insurance if the agreement isn't properly prepared. The solicitor should also be able to raise any necessary enquiries or searches and check the title to the property is free from any defects. These points are particularly important when you plan to spend a great deal of money on the property during the option period.

Does the Seller Need a Separate Solicitor?

You should insist that the seller has legal representation. If the seller refuses to use a solicitor, you cannot force him to do so but you should insist he signs a letter addressed to you acknowledging that you have recommended he seeks legal advice before signing the option, that he has had sufficient time to consider taking advice and that he has decided to sign the documents of his own free will and not under the undue influence of anyone.

Does the Seller Need to Use a Specialist Options Solicitor?

The seller will need to use a solicitor who understands option agreements. Many residential conveyancers will never have dealt with an option agreement, although this isn't true of all. Nearly all commercial property lawyers will be comfortable advising on an option agreement, so you should be able to find a suitable solicitor in most parts of England or Wales.

Chapter 34: Treating it Like a Business

Managing your Property Business

It is important to consider your property portfolio as a business and to run it as such. Brad Sugars, founder of the world's largest business coaching franchise, describes a business:

"My definition of a business is a commercial, profitable enterprise that works without me."

This means if you call the office on Monday morning to say that you are not coming in, things should still run smoothly.

Systems and Processes

The most valuable thing you can do with your time is to build a high positive cash-flowing portfolio. This is then times easier if you're not dealing with tenant and maintenance issues. You will need systems and processes to ensure everything runs efficiently and so that anyone who is doing work for you knows what to do. I'm not an expert so I recommend you read:

The Four Hour Work Week, by Tim Ferris

The E-myth, by Michael Gerber

My advice is to keep systems simple and understandable then continually improve them as you learn.

Building a Team

Ideally you want the processes and systems so good that an untrained person could follow them. If you want to be the best, however, you will need a great team in place. I'm fortunate enough to have a well-motivated team in place that produces excellent results. Recently on my way to Morocco I received an alert on my phone about a property that was for sale. Not wanting to miss out I sent my builder and letting manager to view the property to check it out. Between them they were able to confirm the work required and the letting potential. Within four hours of contacting the agent and while on the tarmac at Luton Airport, I closed the deal worth £1,500 per month profit. That was enough to pay the monthly maintenance and lettings team's wages bill. That's the importance of having a great team! When building a team it is important to focus on attitude rather than skill; skills can be taught whereas attitude cannot. It's also very important to consider your own weaknesses so that you can build a team around them and compliment your strengths.

Become a Great Leader

I cannot emphasise enough that getting a great team is the most important thing here. Once that team is in place you will need to become an effective leader. This involves giving clear instructions, providing systems and processes and then investing time into training them. Once the team member has been trained and has some experience it is important to make them responsible for their role. For example, if a team member approaches you for advice I would suggest initially asking them what they think they should do. This will not only encourage them to think for themselves, but they will also feel valued and therefore more fulfilled. Most people will have a good idea about what should be done but may not have the confidence or the authority to take the decisive action required. It is important to also share your views and experience of the problem based on your own knowledge to ensure you get the best outcome. Remember that you are still 100% responsible for your business.

Get Out of the Way

Since I also have a successful lease options training business I find that I am out of the office more and more. Whilst training others I am fully focused on helping them reach their targets and I am therefore not normally available to my own team during these periods. This means that anything requiring my input cannot be completed immediately and I could stop the business moving forward. It has therefore been necessary to remove myself wherever possible from the day to day running of my property business to allow things to run smoothly. I have done this by empowering the team to make decisions for themselves. The great by-product of this is that I gain more and more freedom. As well as being financially free I can now run my property business with minimal input.

Chapter 35: A Quick Recap on Our Strategy

Here's a quick recap on exactly what we're doing to make options work on great properties and how you can do it too.

Golden Rules for Ethical Investing

- Must be true win–win.
- Aim to give the seller a monthly option fee that is greater than the interest they would receive if they sold the property and put the capital in the bank.
- Aim to ensure that the option fee will cover the mortgage payment.
- Aim to ensure that the purchase price will cover the mortgage redemption figure as a minimum.

Sourcing (Estate and Letting Agents)

Many of our properties are sourced through estate agents and letting agents. Sourcing this way is a great way to leverage other people's time. If you can successfully communicate the benefits of lease options to estate agents and letting agents you can get them to bring properties to you rather than continually searching yourself. Lots of investors tend to steer clear of estate agent and wouldn't even consider letting agents but these sources represent over 90% of the property sales market.

So how do you do this through Estate Agents?

We generally find a property that we think a lease option could work well for and book a viewing. Following the viewing we do some more research into the rental figures achievable and work out the figures for fees, refurbishment, etc. We then put an offer in writing detailing the benefits to the agents, the benefits to the seller and finish with a paragraph telling them about us. We do this to build credibility so we talk about our experience in property, our portfolio of multi-let properties and the fact that we run the Bristol PIN meeting. We take in the written proposal to the estate agent and talk through what we'd like to do and the benefits. We answer any questions and give them the written proposal. We then also offer to email the agents the proposal. We do this as it's the easiest way to get our proposal directly to the seller rather than a diluted version based on what the agent remembers. If the seller is at all interested we arrange a meeting with the agent present. Regardless of whether we do the deal on not, if the agent is keen and understands the benefits of lease options we arrange a meeting to present lease options and all the reasons somebody might like to sell this way. The majority of investors focus solely on people with no equity or negative equity. During the meeting we present eight reasons why a vendor may want to sell this way.

So how do you do this through Letting Agents?

We concentrate on properties that we can multi-let and offer landlords a long term lease. Importantly we offer letting agents a finder's fee because the deal needs to be worthwhile for them. Letting agents agreeing to put forward a lease option are essentially giving up the opportunity to get repeat business from the property. By concentrating on properties that you can increase the rent through multi-letting, you don't need to negotiate down the lease as much.

Our Business Model at a Glance

- High quality properties.
- Desirable areas.
- Large rooms.
- En suites where possible, otherwise a maximum of three to four people to a bathroom.
- Minimum profit £100 per room per month.

- Cost of the option (fees and refurbishment) to be repaid from first year's profit, i.e. 100%.
- Purchase price is today's market value.
- Average term five to seven years (may be less if significant value can be added through refurbishment).
- Rent rooms to students or young professionals (we don't mix these).
- Use parental guarantors to protect income.

Funding for Refurbishment

We offer good rates of return for cash rich investors who don't have the time or inclination to invest themselves. These investors generally have cash generating businesses or high paid jobs. Their time is better spent in their area of passion and expertise rather than taking the time required to become a property professional. The investment is usually secured against one of our owned properties or against the option itself. In the instance where the funds are secured against the option, there is an agreement written up which states that the option will be assigned to the investor if we are unable to repay the loan in line with the agreed terms. The options create good cash-flow and if funds have been borrowed for refurbishment there is usually also equity within the option (the difference between the agreed option price and refurbished value). If we were unable to get investment as described above we would consider a joint venture with an equity share.

Exercising the Option – Buying the Properties

It's difficult to predict what the lending market will be like next week let alone in four to six years' time. We expect lenders to relax their criteria when there is sustained growth within the property market. To be safe we are assuming the lending market will be similar to what it is now. This means we will need a deposit fund of about £300,000 to £400,000 to buy the properties at the end of the option periods in case we need to invest four deposits at any one time. This fund will be recycled as we will be buying the properties below market value (because they are likely to have increased in value above the agreed purchase price) and refinancing three to six months later, using that money to buy the next property. As options are only one of our strategies, we also have a portfolio of owned properties that is continually growing. We plan to refinance this portfolio to raise funds for the purchase deposits. If we need more funds we are confident that we can raise these through private financing. The areas and properties we invest in are very desirable and therefore will be a very safe investment for cash rich investors.

Chapter 36: How to Kick Start your Property Options Portfolio

There is enough material in this book to get you well on your way with building your portfolio. If you would like to kick start your property investing, why not come and spend some time with us?

One Day Courses

With so many people seeing the benefits of investing using options and wanting some help to get going, we have developed a one-day course to get people started. During the day we not only tell people exactly what they need to say to estate agents and letting agents, we get everyone doing role plays and then whilst the energy is really high, actually get people to call agents then and there. Whereas most one day courses are designed solely to get you to sign up to bigger and more expensive courses, ours are designed to get results right there in the room. If you've ever been to a course I'm sure you will recall leaving feeling amazing and like nothing will stop you getting the result. You'll also recall how that buzz quickly dissipates as you get on with your day to day life. People actually walk away from our courses with appointments set up for them to meet agents to discuss using leases and lease options to generate cash-flow. Taking action on the day kick starts people's investing and as a result we have helped many people generate thousands of pounds' income from just this course.

Kathryn and Alan attended our course in February 2012 and within six months they had secured four leases and one lease option. Here's what happened in Kathryn's words:

Kathryn and Alan's Case Study

My partner Alan and I began our investment journey by putting all our money into a one-bedroom flat in Southampton, which came with tenants and gave us £200 income per month (which we thought was amazing). This flat still ticks on along well today, one-and-a-half years later. Today we have annual turnover of £129,300 and net income of £32,000 per year. We have achieved this between April and November 2012 from rent to rents and a lease option.

This new path started when we attended a Simon Zutshi one-day course and I signed up for the year-long Mastermind course. We had the view that we would find investors, buy BMV and within a year start a family and not have to work. Well after five months, we had no investors, were trying lots of ways to find BMV properties, but all we had concluded was that we were persistent and this strategy was tough in our area. In February 2012 I attended a session with Barry and his business partner Ben and was inspired. On meeting them again, they agreed that we could attend their one-day rent to rent course and managed to negotiate a BMV deal on the price, on the promise that we would take massive action.

The morning of the course, we were both tired, rowed as we didn't really want to travel to Birmingham again but headed up the M40 to see what Ben and Barry would teach. The day was great, we won the dream-board* competition which meant that we had an hour of coaching with both Barry and Ben individually. After the course we set about finding rent to rent properties and after three weeks and forty-one viewings we got our first break:

First Deal – Holly Drive

Monthly rent	£1,200
Monthly cost (bills and investor)	£416
Gross monthly rental income	£2,140
Net monthly income	£524

All of our deals have virtually none of our own money left in. Our monthly costs include paying back investors' capital and interest at 40% over three years. We feel we have a win-win for our landlords, investors and tenants.

In these seven months we have taken on four rent to rent properties and a lease option deal all within Berkshire. The lease option came from a letting agent we now work with a lot. The property had been renovated by the vendor and had been on the market for nine months and not sold. As soon as it came up for rent we went to see it and placed two offers to the landlord/vendor via the letting agent; one being a rent to rent and the other a lease option. To our surprise and delight the lease option was accepted!

Our Lease Option Deal – Blackamoor Lane

5-year option to purchase for £250,000 (the property is worth about £235,000 today).

Option fee	£1,725
Monthly fee	£1,150
Monthly costs	£416
Gross monthly rental income	£2,070
Net monthly income	£504

Our plan is to stick with rent to rent and lease options deals for twelve months until April 2013. This will create a base for our future and I have already given in my resignation at work and will leave on 31st March 2013. Our target is to find a minimum of five more rent to rents between January and March 2013, which will give us approximately £250,000 turnover and a net income of £64,000 per year.

This journey has been and still is a roller-coaster ... there have been huge highs and massive lows, but when we have experienced difficult times, we have been lucky to have friends in our property network like Barry to call on, who listened hard, gave sound advice and sent a motivating YouTube clip! We believe that persistence is key to achieving results and having belief in the things we have learnt through our property education are becoming a reality and worth every effort.

Kathryn Owen

Mentoring – Working with Estate Agents

We are constantly updating and improving our mentoring to keep up to date with the market. At the time of writing this book our mentoring follows the structure below.

Mentoring Pack

- What is a lease option contract and how is it constructed?
- How much to pay.
- How to calculate the maximum lease fee you can afford to pay.
- How long should you have the option for?
- How much upfront option fee you should pay?
- How to structure win-win deals.
- A detailed explanation of the eight reasons someone might want to sell using lease options.
- Tips on how to negotiate great deals.

Initial Homework

- Read "The art of the deal" or "Think big and kick ass", both by Donald Trump.
- Create a dream board of what you want in your life.
- Complete the pre-mentoring questionnaire.

Lesson One

I teach you one-to-one, the eight reasons someone might sell using options and how to present this to estate agents.

Homework

You learn and practice the presentation ready to give it to the estate agents

Lesson Two

You present to me as if I were an estate agent. I make notes of what went well and a few things that we can improve and we work on those areas and role-play those parts of the presentation again.

Homework

Practice the presentation and adapt to match your style and your requirements.

Lesson Three

We calculate how to make an offer based on the achievable rent. We work through how to put an offer into writing and then how to present this to the estate agent. We search Rightmove for properties in your area that we believe would be great for lease options.

Homework

Preparation for the big day!

You arrange appointments to view four to six of the properties selected. Ideally you would view them two to four days prior to the on-site part of the mentoring. You then make appointments to go in to chat to the estate agents about the properties that you have viewed. The appointments need to be made for the on-site mentoring day.

For each property:

- Research the achievable rent for each property.
- Calculate an offer for each property that you are interested in acquiring through options.
- Use the offer letter template to put each offer into writing.
- Book an appointment to speak in person to each agent for each property you wish to acquire.

The Big Day – Template Schedule

9.00 Tea / coffee time – last minute queries answered.
9.30 First appointment – Barry beautifully presents (Client interjects occasionally).
10.15 Debrief – what went well? What did you learn? What are you still unsure of?
11.00 Second appointment – Barry the Great presents (client interjects more occasionally).

11.45 Debrief – what went well? What did you learn? What are you still unsure of? Which parts of the presentation would you like me to cover when you lead the next presentation?

12.30 Great presentation by the client, perfectly backed up by Barry.

13.15 Celebration lunch! What went well? Should we change anything? Take time out to relax and reflect on successes.

14.30 Great presentation by the client, less input from Barry.

15.15 Debrief – what went well? How could you be even better?

16.00 Last presentation – Client smashes it.

16.45 All tea'd out we get a quick beer or wine.

The Fortune is in the Follow Up

Clients' first homework is to follow up as agreed in agent presentation meetings. This includes following up on the offers put forward and viewing other potential properties discussed with the agents. The week after the meeting we have a coaching call to discuss the results of the day and further actions required. Further coaching calls arranged by the client as required for up to six weeks.

Mentoring – Working with Letting Agents

- We tell you exactly what to say to get option deals from letting agents.
- We provide you with the script that has worked time and time again.
- We give you the most frequently asked objections and how to handle them.
- We role-play to ensure you know how to get agents to give you property after property.
- We support you in calling the agents.
- We view properties with you to ensure they are suitable.

"Barry came down for the day ... he helped me build relationships with estate agents which meant that I got two deals from estate agents straight away from that. It just gave me all the confidence to go back into other agents. For me it's not just those two deals, it's all of the rest of the deals in the future.... Cash-flow (profit) will be £780 from the first one and £900 from the second."

Rachael Wilson, Winner MM8

To see Rachael's full video please visit:

http://www.youtube.com/watch?feature=player_emb edded&v=7_MZdKa7SYs

Chapter 37: Bonus Section – What to Do when Options don't Work

Since options are just one tool I thought it would be good to give a couple of case studies of other deals I've done when options don't work. Many people will be using lease option either because they can't get a mortgage or because they don't have the money to invest in the deposit. This is the exact position I was in when I did the deals in the case studies below.

Kingswood, Bristol

An option deal was sold to me by another Masterminder. I had viewed the property and valued it for him (this is one of the great things about Simon's Mastermind – everyone helps each other), and because of this I was given first refusal on the deal. I was happy to buy the deal; a lot of people on Mastermind feel that with all the education they have they shouldn't buy deals. I think their ego is getting in the way – a deal is a deal! I went round to sign the paperwork with the seller and he was nowhere to be seen. I called him, he answered but said he had changed his mind, an option wasn't for him.

This was fine; I wouldn't want anyone to do something they weren't 100% happy with. I had a chat with the guy who created the deal and suggested it would be worth following up (it's always worth following up). The seller was going on holiday the next day and I didn't want to hassle him. I decided to write him a letter re-offering the option and also an offer for a fast purchase. The offer for the fast purchase was for £104,000. The property was worth £130,000 (20% discount) and with £2,000 spent on refurbishment it would be worth £140,000. The purchase offer was accepted, we fulfilled our side of the bargain by completing within five weeks and the seller walked away happy.

We quickly refurbished the house and rented it for six months before deciding to sell.

Despite regularly using the current 'buyers' market' to my advantage I failed to realise that the property might be hard to sell. It took nearly six months to sell and we ended selling at a reduced price of £136,500. Incidentally we didn't use any of our own money or even get the mortgage in our own name. Instead we used a mortgage host and funds from two investors'. After interest and mortgaging fees, hosting fees (£3,000) were paid we made a profit of £20,500.

What have you learned from this case study?

_____

_____

_____

_____

_____

_____

What key actions can you take as a result of your learning?

_____

_____

_____

_____

_____

_____

Southmead, Bristol

This case study is a lesson in persistence. I had first made contact with this seller two years before agreeing and completing a deal. They were in negative equity (the outstanding mortgage was worth more than the house) so I suggested an option, but for some reason they were not keen on this idea. We kept in contact and he asked what I would be willing to pay for a quick sale.

The house was valued at £125,000 to £135,000. The outstanding balance of the mortgage and a secured loan was £137,000. I told him that for a quick sale I could pay £100,200. Somehow he managed to unsecure the loan and negotiate for the bank to accept a low settlement figure for the mortgage meaning that we were able to complete the transaction at £101,000. The best bit about the deal was that the property, although ex-council, was close to a major hospital and other large employers. This meant we were able to multi-let the property for a great profit.

Summary of the Deal

Initial Figures
Deposit and refurbishment: £30,000
Total rentable rooms: 5
Average rent: £335 per room
Total rent: £1,685
Mortgage: £293
Bills: £350
Total monthly profit: £1,042

This property was re-mortgaged twelve months later and we were able to borrow based on the value (£125,000) rather than the purchase price. We borrowed 80% of the value of the property so the new mortgage was £100,000. This enabled us to withdraw £29,500 (all but £500 of our initial investment). The property now produces £890 cash-flow/profit per month even though we now only have £500 invested in it.

What have you learned from this case study?

_____

_____

_____

_____

_____

_____

What key actions can you take as a result of your learning?

_____

_____

_____

_____

_____

_____

Chapter 38: My Next Steps

The Year Ahead!

My most recent learnings are that I should focus as much of my time as possible doing what I enjoy, what I'm best at and what is most valuable to the company. For me this is doing deals, growing the portfolio and sharing my knowledge. The first two work together well since doing great deals allows me to invest in property without using my own money. This in turn means that I can grow the portfolio indefinitely. In the immediate future the goal is to use private investment to fund deals. Within a year I expect the portfolio to be self-funding where the monthly cash-flow is enough to pay the deal being done that month. Then as the cash-flow grows through the new properties bought, a fund is built to buy the properties at the end of the option term.

To enable me to grow I need to move away from the areas of the business that I am least good at or passionate about. For example, I love the idea that we provide the best accommodation and the best service to our young professional and student tenants and I am already proud when students come to view the properties and say that it's the best they have seen. Does that mean that I'm passionate about delivering that service personally? Certainly not! Am I good at dealing with tenants? Not particularly good. Is dealing with tenants the best use of my time? No, I should be out doing deals that increase the company cash-flow by £500 a month or more.

I also know the more that we can systemise the business, the better it will perform and the greater the profit. Again, I'm not passionate about delivering systems, I'm not great at it and it's not the best use of my time.

Our future growth therefore will come from developing an experienced team. I'm confident that I can find someone who will love to make the tenants' experience the best that it can be. I also believe that we can charge a premium for this service. I'm also sure that we will find someone who would love to systemise our business to make it as efficient as possible. By the end of the year we will have close to 100 tenants and therefore if we can provide a better service and charge £20 month more per room, we will increase cash-flow by £2,000 a month. And if through systemising and improving efficiency we can save £10 per room per month we will save £1,000 per month.

Mentoring is massively rewarding for me. Personally there is no better feeling than helping someone to unleash their potential. I've had a number of mentors myself and have found their input invaluable. It's great to be able to share experiences with people who are going through exactly the kind of thing that we have been through. In minutes you can answer questions that would have taken them days to research themselves. It's also great to give clients simple and effective tools for calculating their property offers, etc. The beauty of mentoring is that it has a holistic effect. For example, one of the key things we work on is confidence around approaching estate agents. Giving someone the confidence to do this successfully also plays out in other areas of their lives.

The Next Ten Years

Having already by far surpassed the expectations that I set for myself when I had a J.O.B. (just over broke) in just three short years, it's hard to imagine what could be achieved in the next three, five or even ten years. One thing I know is that I've always wanted to do better. Starting with small two- or three-bedroom terraces in cheap parts of town I soon set my sights higher. I had been to a seminar by Joseph McClendon, part of which was about goal setting. The homework for the first night was to write a goal, to describe in detail how it would feel when you had achieved the goal and to draw a picture or find an image of that goal. Back then, not knowing how it could be achieved, I set the goal of having a multi-million pound portfolio of good quality properties in desirable areas. I have now achieved that goal and have gained massive experience and confidence along the way.

Looking forward, it's hard to imagine what's possible. Reading Donald Trump's books "The Art of The Deal" and "Think Big and Kick Ass" has inspired me to think much bigger. Strolling to Bristol City Centre (about five to 10 minutes from my house) one summer's evening last year, I was walking past the beautiful seven hundred year old cathedral and one hundred year old library. Ahead I could see a chic modern tall skyscraper. This was a great vision of how new and old could work well together. Bristol is a great city with a great deal of history and architecture. What is sadly missing is good modern architecture (there are a few 1970's monstrosities around). On this beautiful summer's evening my imagination started to get the better of me. Was I the person to create great modern buildings in the centre of Bristol? Watch this space.

The Long Term Goal

My long term goal is to become a Billionaire. Why, you may ask? You could never spend that kind of money. In the words of Donald Trump

"Money was never a big motivation for me, except as a way to keep score. The real excitement is playing the game."

Donald Trump

Money is just a good way of keeping score, I guess. There is a part of all high achievers that wants to win and a billion is a good win, but that's all ego driven. The deeper reason is that a billion is a good legacy. My aim is to create a foundation or donate to an existing foundation. £1 billion invested well should produce £50 to £100 million a year through interest and dividends. Provided that the original billion is never spent this £50 to £100 million would be donated to good causes every year forever! Within ten to twenty years of the foundation being set up it would have donated £1 billion to charity through interest alone and the foundation would keep producing.

About the Author

Barry Davies is a professional property investor, coach and mentor. Barry has achieved financial freedom through the multi million pound property portfolio that he has grown over the four years preceding the writing of this book.

Barry is passionate about property investing and loves doing property deals. Whilst most investors are content doing deals on properties worth less than £100,000, Barry continuously looks for bigger and better deals to inspire himself and those around him. His biggest deal will be worth £550,000 when the works of his latest project are complete and he is now in search of a £1,000,000 deal. Barry finds smaller property deals uninspiring and believes that work should be both fun and inspiring.

Barry has run the Bristol PIN (property investors network) meeting with his best friend and business partner for two-and-a-half years. Running the meeting puts Barry at the centre of the local hub for property investors.

Keeping physically fit is paramount to Barry. He weight trains two to three times a week, does fitness training twice a week and pays rugby regularly during the rugby season. He is keen to give any sport or challenge a go and is always looking for more experiences.

Barry loves to help others achieve their property and financial targets. For many people, taking leases on property with the exclusive option to purchase during the lease period is the best way to financial freedom. To Barry, financial freedom means not having to go to work. The many case studies in the book show how Barry has helped people on their way to financial freedom through his mentorship programme.

Barry continues to follow his passion and still invests to achieve bigger and better goals. Barry loves what he does and has no plans to retire.

Extra Resources

barrydaviesproperty.co.uk

barry@barrydaviesproperty.co.uk

facebook.com/HMOLeaseOptions

http://www.youtube.com/watch?feature=player_emb
edded&v=uXbKGL9cXFs

One day Let to Let and Multi-let Options seminar:

http://www lettoletquickstart.co.uk

My business partner's peak performance coaching site
The League of Warriors

http://www theleagueofwarriors.com

Action List

"An ounce of action is worth a ton of theory."

Ralph Waldo Emerson

Action No.	Description	Date
1		
2		
3		
4		
5		
6		
7		
8		
9		
10		
11		
12		
13		
14		
15		
16		
17		
18		
19		
20		